SO RECENTLY RENT A WORLD

SO REC-ENTLY RENT A WORLD

NEW AND SELECTED POEMS: 1968–2012

Andrei Codrescu

COFFEE HOUSE PRESS
MINNEAPOLIS
2012

COFFEE HOUSE PRESS books are available to the trade through our primary distributor, Consortium Book Sales & Distribution, cbsd.com or (800) 283-3572. For personal orders, catalogs, or other information, write to: info@coffeehousepress.org.

Coffee House Press is a nonprofit literary publishing house. Support from private foundations, corporate giving programs, government programs, and generous individuals helps make the publication of our books possible. We gratefully acknowledge their support in detail in the back of this book. To you and our many readers around the world, we send our thanks for your continuing support.

Good books are brewing at coffeehousepress.org.

LIBRARY OF CONGRESS CIP INFORMATION
Codrescu, Andrei, 1946–
So recently rent a world : new and selected poems / by Andrei Codrescu.
p. cm.
Includes bibliographical references.
ISBN 978-1-56689-300-8 (pbk. : alk. paper)
ISBN 978-1-56689-304-6 (trade cloth : alk. paper)
1. Title.
PS3553.O386 2012
811'.54—DC23
2012027229
PRINTED IN THE UNITED STATES
1 3 5 7 9 8 6 4 2
FIRST EDITION | FIRST PRINTING

The author is grateful to the publishers and editors who first took notice of these poems and loosed them into the world: Arif Press, Big Table/Follett, Black Sparrow Press, George Braziller, Capra Press, Coffee House Press, Cymric Press, Four Zoas Press, Grape Press, Panjandrum Press, and Tree Books. The author would also like to express his gratitude to the many literary magazines—too numerous to name here—that published his work during the last forty-plus years.

SO RECENTLY RENT A WORLD

NEW POEMS

1 signifier

3 ars poetica for ludwig zeller

5 ars polis

7 history and (poetry) class

11 blue jew notes

14 david franks

17 driving

18 essay

20 eulogy for men

21 new market

23 so?

24 five one-minute eggs

27 french quarter morning

28 do innocents exist?

29 the gulf of mexico (social realism)

33 how it happened

34 "if you're news you're meat" CNN

35 bridge work

36 master manole to anna

40 the new millenium

41 a redaction

42 salt

43 "keep old hat in secret closet"

46 sentenced to the frost

48 sweat the small stuff

50 torture and evolution

53 life haikus

56 EU or the poetry of menus

58 haifa

59 they will do whatever it takes

60 one syllable

61 translation

62 strangled memory

63 the avant-garde then and now

65 two threats for joel dailey's fell swoop

67 foolish things to do immediately

68 5.14.2012 facebook redux

70 the gap

71 a petite epic for the lovejoy ramp

79 accents (a night in new orleans)

81 the ballad of generous hariette

84 e. a. poe at the university of baltimore

86 a heroic odelle to john on his birthday

87 new orleans art for wall street 2004

89 birthday poem & bed frame IOU for my love 9.27.2001

90 rain

91 blackout

92 russian story

94 ode to allen ginsberg

PERSONAE: LICENSE TO CARRY A GUN

97 introduction

JULIO HERNANDEZ

100 untitled ("there is an orange . . .")
101 from a trilogy of birds
102 untitled ("i'm careful . . .")
103 untitled ("melville knew me . . .")
104 green
105 blue
106 leadership

ALICE HENDERSON-CODRESCU

108 beach near sebastopol california
109 zzzzzzzzzzzzz
110 reverse
111 dream dogs
112 new jersey
113 debts

PETER BOONE

115 all wars are holy
116 note
117 the flag
118 after meng
119 testing. testing.
120 gist

THE HISTORY OF THE GROWTH OF HEAVEN

123 introduction

125 face portrait

126 new york

127 trains

128 a grammar

129 early fix

130 opium for britt wilkie

131 opium for archie anderson

132 crossed hands

133 about photography

134 the good spirit

135 history

136 why write

137 fear

139 san francisco for whomever

140 late night san francisco

141 thieves seasons

142 new morning

THE CHAPBOOKS I

145 introduction

THE HISTORY OF THE GROWTH OF HEAVEN

147 Dear Editors

148 the holy grail

149 my next book

150 symmetry

151 the indecent assumption, the slaughter songs

152 the status of the monk

153 a programme for the double-barrel life when it hits

154 junk mail

155 souls looking for bodies

A SERIOUS MORNING

156 the imagination of necessity

157 looks from money

158 saturnian dilemma

159 tête-à-tête

& GRAMMAR & MONEY

160 grammar

161 here

162 5 ways of saying the same thing

163 & power

164 dollar dance

SECRET TRAINING

165 three types of loss

169 2 plays

170 on translation

171 biographical notes

172 de natura rerum

FOR MAX JACOB

173 bilingual

174 les fleurs du cinéma

175 evening particulier

176 port of call

177 mail

178 the wallpaper of mr. r.k.

THE CHAPBOOKS II

181 introduction

THE MARRIAGE OF INSULT AND INJURY

183 talking through my hat

185 to my heart

186 the yes log

187 the differences

191 the park

193 old cities

194 a cook in hell

202 the marriage of insult and injury

THE LADY PAINTER

204 avanti

205 the lady painter

206 the penal cavalry

207 the monk

208 center piece

209 toward the end of 1969

210 in the supermarket

211 stock report

FOR THE LOVE OF A COAT

212 selavie

213 a good thing when i see one

214 à francis ponge

215 ode to curiosity

216 untitled ("MAN" and "WOMAN" . . .)

217 sunday sermon

218 untitled ("It takes joy . . .")

219 the goldrush

220 talking

221 the threat

222 epitaph

NECROCORRIDA

223 en face

224 wishes

225 love & the documents

226 the new gazette

227 the discovery of prayer

228 staying with it

229 the gambling phoenix

230 irony as nursery

231 working for profit

232 matinée

233 against meaning

234 model work

235 drizzle off the ocean

236 paper on humor

ALIEN CANDOR

239   introduction

241   a game

242   your country

243   "the woods" at midnight

244   old photo

245   the origin of electricity

246   talismanic ceremony for lucian

248   poetry

249   getting there

250   orbital complexion

251   slot-o-topia

254   every tie

256   a petite histoire of red fascism

258   not a pot to piss in

COMRADE PAST & MISTER PRESENT

277 introduction

279 dear masoch

288 the fourth of july

295 music

300 petite madeleine

302 comrade past & mister present

BELLIGERENCE

319 introduction

321 belligerence

323 another globe

326 leaves of nerves

327 demands of exile

329 intention

334 christmas in new york

338 a leafy angel

IT WAS TODAY

343 introduction

LU LI AND WENG LI

345 introduction

346 Lu Li

351 Weng Li

357 Coda

358 nickelodeon

359 to poetry

360 the portuguese eat a dish

361 old snake ponders

362 my name is andrei codrescu

364 my son came over

366 as tears go by

368 often after a public event

369 brâncuși's fish

371 the revolution and the poet

372 in jerusalem on my 48th birthday

375 the view from the baby seat

JEALOUS WITNESS

383 introduction

385 did something miss new orleans?

386 the mold song

388 in the picture above

389 topiary

391 visitors from the dancing world

393 walnuts

395 tristan tzara the man who said no

397 the incoming sneeze or the old man's nose

398 desk 07 in the reading room at the british library

401 legacy: letters

404 the zen post office

406 present at the ceremony

407 in memory of the 20th century

NEW POEMS

signifier

One day I had an idea.
This I you don't know.
This I I barely knows.

Choosing some things and leaving out others was largely decided by
the disposition of my first person singular. It's a nearly half-century
journey from the defiant "I" of my early poems in Romanian to the
instrumental "I" of my latest. The road passes through the unstable "I"
of personae who were not "me" in both Romanian and English; it
suffers the indignities of personal injuries and biographical incidents;
it references itself in philosophical quandaries; it digs itself out of
unspoken agreements; it borrows, burrows, lends, and exclaims, and
(occasionally) gives itself a talking to. At the age of sixteen or so, in
Romanian, the person speaking employs its "I" to declare the presence
of a poet whose intention is to set himself against the accepted first-
person singular of any authority, parental or statal. This is an "I" that
is mostly spontaneous but also borrowed like the shell of a hermit crab
from lyric rebels like Villon, Rimbaud, Blaga, and Arghezi. The hard-
headedness of this "I" is scary, a reckless plunge that dares the law to
spare the speaker from public execution because of his (medieval)
ability to read, a skill that covered loosely the alibi of personality
against whatever felony was committed. The assumption that author-
ity made no distinction between the obscure facts of personal experi-
ence and imaginary settings for sentiment, would have been tragic (as
it indeed was for many 20th-century poets) if it hadn't been also comic
and fresh. The speaker was nobody, an "I" who staged his poetry with

the music of sounds that fascinated it. On the other hand, this was an "I" that posed a challenge to law and decorum with the coy proviso, "I am only speaking for myself and people like myself, of course, and how many of us sick fucks can there be?" (Many, as it turned out when they gave a revolution). In the u.s., my adolescent Romanian "I" met the emerging political "fuck you" of the 1960's. What happens after that is in English, and the story of this book.

ars poetica for ludwig zeller

The cool view by the cooler
Was of altă mărie cu aceeași pălărie.
Saying thank you with words I've already said
for this prize that recognizes what I already wrote
makes me feel very old, like having a flashback
of a déjà-vu in a play I acted in for years.
It's no easy job producing miracles
out of the curiosity of others for others
but mostly from and for your own curiosity
about the curious others in the sieve of your curious self.
At ten my Nobel acceptance speech was incredible
And I probably won't get it until I remember it.
I have received the Ovid prize for succeeding
in returning, something Ovid only did postmortem.
Anselm Hollo in his poem "Uncle O" predicted this thing.
Most people remember just enough to structure
the story of their own life but some people remember more
to patch up those huge whistling holes.
Returning a book in France can be a nightmare
like an etch-a-sketch, said my art student, I do it every night.
Why don't you just keep it? I suggested.
Because it's the only book the French can't do without.
Keeping it would cause a national collapse.
What is this book? I was astonished that such a book
existed in France where there are many good books
without which some of the countries where they'd been translated
would collapse for lack of lyric support.
That's the thing, she said, I don't know, I wake up.

There is no peril that my book just published in French is that book, I reassured her.

ars polis

the frequency of portraits in postmortem inventories
in the 17th to the 18th century grows from 18 to 28 percent
while the percentage of religious portraits falls from 29 to
   12 percent
—george vigarello

way too human too fast way too boring too quick
the wrong humans at that
humans that tick like clocks
the saints were in no hurry

nor the poor

every time a slum is being abolished
peoples' right to get fucked up
is abridged
more immortality ground up like beef

display patties in square windows

no streets to perform on
no place to squat for a good shell game

OTB poetry parlor where are you?

poetry that good superstition
guessing where the third pea hides
anybody can play

you can't be a bit superstitious
and a bit rational
a little in a book and a little outside

but you can keep betting
and never guessing

and when they explain everything on TV
japanese woman arrested for killing virtual husband
on the crawl that used to be the street

you walk three frustrated miles
meeting no one you know no one who knows you
you could swear it's the same place where you had
hundreds of friends and acquintances
the buildings haven't moved
you never find out where the party is

> *the gaze doesn't reveal anything*
> *it places us instantly in a different situation*
> —victor brauner

no point in looking for it
it's not the past or the wrong city
it's your transparent body

sola la muerte es fuerte

only death is 100% proof

history and (poetry) class

yelping for the proletariat
it must be the 30s
that's walker evans
and that's diego in detroit
everybody on the train is reading
a USSR travel book

that was in the 20th century
it's 2010 now the bourgeoisie can only achieve contentment
through the unhapiness of artists who can wreck that contentment
through ecstasy

suffering artists are promoted to the expense of ecstatics (and mystics!)
we are at the ceremony but pretend to be elsewhere

which is what the tretyakov galleries meant to say all along

class, analyze the 20th century in the following keys:
1. freud
2. jung
3. marx
4. fashion
5. the kabbalah
6. the news
7. art
8. advertising
9. the future
10. the assignment

i would rather be in you than with you
but here we are artists and analysts all mixed up
like parts of the gun each one of you has been assigned
at the beginning of your (social) class

pay attention: this is the clip
every thought symmetry
    what sounds
      what you hear
            matter
                each bullet is "you"

the imperative is to think in piano keys
that are actually bullets

this man with the shovel is a digger
I found him on the vacant lot as I was looking
        for something to bring to show-and-tell
when I found him he had just finished digging
a new rift
    in american education
        a trench
and now class he will dig something for you
            he'll find the interstices
    in the trenches he's digging
that's where the candy is hidden
        (in your machine guns)

the earth might collapse on him
whatever happens don't move
keep breaking down and putting back together
your gun your clip your life your ambitions

this terrain is made for you and me
even if it looks like belgium at first

it's both narrative and complicated
but it moves forward

load your gadgets
    and note how fast he digs your grave
fear of heights doesn't matter
        when you're in this deep

                        *

last week's assignment: *invent poet*
Here is a good one from Mrs. Ohio I'll read it out loud:

Hannah Temmett lives in Barcelona. She works as an assistant to
film director Pedro Almodovar. She has published a bilingual poetry
collection, *Telesintesa* (Libros Jose Corti) I read it, translated it,
emailed it to the class, I hope it's a third of my grade. Here is an
example of Ms. Temmett's work:

Mira

pierced tangent
  named quickly
oblique or furtive
  "I know you"
no you don't yes I do
play pinochle
    with this reed
      with those lips
pitched roof so steep the dark
    tastes soft like you

9

Hanna Temmett lives in Barcelona with her girlfriend of three years, Elena. One day she goes to the temp office and she's sent to a sound studio on Avenida x to do office work for a couple of guys making a soundtrack for a film by Pedro Almodovar's nephew Corinto. She shows Pedro her poetry.

A+

there are a lot of poets and you must meet them all
        I have.

there is only a slight vowel difference between fetal and fatal
        that difference is YOU

                        discuss
also discuss
if buzzards had $ would they eat carryout
            (goes for crows too)

                    discuss also
are crystal amber and ginger the three muses of the strip mall?

        and this:
            is adam a typo?

you up front: manipulate the word
        it doesn't move by itself

here are some things *I* learned:

most people are fat and violent.
no generalization without penetration.
if you can see it on TV you don't need it in a book.
communism didn't collapse, it exploded like elvis.
clitoris-weller cliff dweller is an oxymoron.

when you have these or different types of learning
        you are me

blue jew notes

7.14.10 new string theorist jokes
gravity is the many ways in which the physical universe can be
wrong. only way to rid us of it is to shake it, shake it, shake it—til
we get it right.

4.5.10 spring is here! the bats are awake!
4.6.10
Are there any holy sites, like Jerusalem, on the internet? Something
we can really fight about? This iPhone capitalizes internet automati-
cally, i had to decapitalise it manually; it thinks it's god. step outside,
motherfucker!

3.30.10 mick vranich died last night

craggy old youth
craggy to the end
no doubt no doubt
detroit constellation
sweet e-mail from stacy aab

in a prior planet

when cars came streaming
into the erogenous zones
of a young world
when death was still dials

we were poets who drove

2.5.10
the dead are grateful to this world
which is why the grateful dead are still alive
and this world is grateful to the dead
for saying what they say

metaphors less apt than comparisons even
because they introduce chronology where there is only continuity

besides only some of the Dead are dead

physical (named, "solid") is the same as mental (polynamed, in flux),
one topos

in the 20th century we feared machines for becoming like people,
and taking over, but in the 21st we have become more like machines,
so we no longer fear them; we perceive them as ideal rather than
scary. They *have* taken over. My body, my machine. The only thing
that stood between our perfect union was psychology, but pills have
gotten rid of it.

(not novels though: they insist: the dead skin of the word)

7.18.10 blue jew at boston diner 2009
a blue jew
a horny jew
a jew with blue balls
an old boston jew
where the snow is blue
the blue-cheese burger
overdone by the black-blue
short-order cook from benares
with the blue elephant inked on her ankle
the sky is blue in benares

the snow is eggplant blue in boston
oh blue jew blue jew
the books are dusty and blue
you read them all when they were new
oh daddy sylvia way outrhymed you

what a difference a few years make! compare the above paeans to dead and live friends with the earlier note below:

friends 8.25.07
robin calls from the city far away
he's in a coffee shop where a woman claiming to be half
my messiah has made her home
and they demand a romanian party next weekend
it entails eating geeen onions from her body
i say "put her on the phone," and sarah says "let's meet next week
      end though I'm tied up most weekends"
so i say "we have to make time to tie you up in some other way"
"e-mail with facts and dates coming pronto," she says
      before hanging up

david franks

since january 31, 2010
for betsy boyd

this world is how the dead communicate
with something neither us nor them

everything sensible is a message from the dead

and everything dead is a message from us
for something beyond them that is beyond us

we are whatever they say
and they are whatever we say

and we know not who we say it to

i'm a letter you're a letter
we crossed in the mail

sealed and going
plain and enigmatic

but just between us we are either here or there
the messages we are not meant for either

machines are how this world communicates with itself
but some machines—like guitars—bring messages from the dead
faster than we here to ourselves

all musical instruments do including the human voice

i said if anybody can get a message thru
david will

so here it is

if you like it here get thee machined
if not
let song wing it

mental geography *is* geography
the same topos as what's out the window
going on named out there and unnamed in the mind

no ideas but in things indeed
including things of the mind

mind topos and geofeatures going on without a break
all of them here and there
both hi tree and what did i just say

the wave of event made of all particles sensible and undetected

it's the stuff that travels back and forth that interests the back *and*
the forth

the messaging

oh and those lips
i put that letter in and then we were three
eros cupid and psyche

on their way somewhere busy busy

or da capo
this world is just what the dead say
not *to* anyone
just talking

do we talk back
oh yes we do

driving

the lie is brief and sweet
the truth is forever and hard
in dry prong louisiana on march 7 2011

the lie can last a long time says laura
you mean like religion
that and other things like that

prisons hospitals churches
simultaneous afterthoughts

only trees seem to be trees
whose inmates didn't build them

Technology is the mechanization of ritual.

For ritual to have any power, new meaning must be added each time
it is performed.

Technology contains only as much meaning as there is at any given time.

When there is sufficient accretion of meaning there is technological
advance.

Take a simple ritual: shaving.

The technology is a shaver, soap, mirror. What the man thinks when
he shaves is new.

If it is really new each time he shaves, at the end of each week he'll
need a new blade.

Newer and better blades are invented all the time to keep up with
the man's beard.

If the man quits thinking his blade becomes duller and duller. One
day he stops shaving.

Take a complex ritual: Transylvanian wedding shouts.

Men slap their belts rhythmically on the ground shouting the names
of the foods they are hoping to eat: stuffed cabbage! polenta with
cheese!

lamb chops! currant pies! cake! baba ghanoush! baklava!

This ritual is festive but also threatening: the chants confirm the joy
of the community at the wedding, and also the threat to eat the hosts
if the guests' culinary standards aren't met. This threat is humorous
but not benign.

Each time the chants are performed all its former forms are
acknowledged:

humor, terror, appetite, and duty to the community layered by irony
(or ironed by many ironic commentaries adding a layer at each
    wedding).
One day a robot shows up with a machine gun: it orders the women
    to cook.
All the irony is gone, and so is the song.
The communal threat has become a machine.
But the baby is still the result of a communal effort
so the demands of the armed robot are reasonable.
He has become human enough to be a retro man.
Now he will invent writing.

eulogy for men

for ruxandra

men have doubles.
women don't.
men invent doubles for women so that they can both have a woman.
women pretend that they too have a double to please their double-man.
women may have many double-men who believe that they have a
    double-woman.
one woman can be the author of dozens of imaginary women for
    their many double-men.
one woman can make many women from stories.
eve had to make up lillith. sheherezade had to make up 1001 women.
but there was only one eve and one sheherezade, the rest were men's
    dreams.
women invented speech to multiply themselves while also multiplying
    men.
women are the mothers of stories and the mothers of men.
poor men whose only gift is to listen and whose only strength is
    being two.

new market

create
twelve facebook gods, name them
after the months
à la révolution française
assign each of them to OCD friends
born in them or temperamentally suited
to the choleric Anusis the melancholy Ursina etc
provide each god with a daily sura
and a lesson for every hour
meant to replace horoscope and toothbrush
for friends who then go forth to friends
suited to their gods

when there are five thousand gods
(the allotted limit per friend)
hope that the five thousand will each
find another five thousand
whose planets elements organs personalities
words clothes preferences recommendations
make a solid pyramid scheme inside the larger pyramid
of facebook itself

then wait for the milk flowing from the pyramid
built from your divinities
it won't take long before your tub will fill with milk
your house with minions your safe with gold
your garden with large ornamental cabbages

turn milk gold minions and cabbages into apps
and seed the internet with them
always leaving a back door to your original twelve gods,
steel-spring doors that snap once the devotee's in

sacramental tools for new cults venture capital needed

so?

Redundancy is nature and technology's insurance policy, good for everything, except language, where it has come to mean something pejorative, though "repetition" and "reiteration" have kept a positive light; to repeat is lyrical, to reiterate good, but to redound, god forbid.

12.14.08 It's fitting that GWB's reign ends with shoes thrown at him, after he made everybody in the world take off their shoes at the aiport. Remember the shoe bomber. The Pakistan riots over shoes in Islamic script. The little red shoes (from blood) we couldn't stop dancing in in Iraq. Spontaneous mass movement rises to throw farewell shoes at Bush in D.C. as he leaves office. If the shoe fits. Size ten.

There is only one subject: the abyss between theory and practice. Only the abyss is interesting: both theory and practice suck.

five one-minute eggs

1. *the economy*

We used to make things we didn't understand (Marx) and consumed by people who didn't understand us, and now we don't even understand the people who are making them, that is us. Our misunderstandings progress.

We consume things that are familiar, and the more familiar they get, the less we know or sympathize with ourselves, the people who make them. We are not familiar with the parts of these things that other people make, but we love to use them. Technology is familiar, people are not. The people who make TVs know us from TV better than we know them or ourselves. When we are not on TV, we are waiting to slit our (their) throats.

Can you love people you don't understand? With a blender and a mixer and an iPhone.
The Jesuits would be pleased.
Why would God need to choose a people with all these machines around?

2. *pound in the ozarks*

5-time grimace:
pro patria
pro domo
pro usura
pro forma
pro pane

3. expansive song

space is my Baby
time is my Bitch

   (with Vince Cellucci's february 2009 Dave Brinks reading)

4. iBroker

   "in this army you break down your body like a gun
   ascertain its needs and reassemble it for action when they've been met"
   —the manual

splitting hairs for commodities
the centrifugal force that dismembers matter into sellable minis

the stockbroker broke down his body and ordered its needs from a catalog
everything arrived by mail overnight and the broker reassembled herm-
   self by the time the market opened
he hoped to make enough to post a profit over the increasing needs of
   herm body
"every day you don't sell you buy"
herm ever-expanding ever-needy body was an expense that had to be
   covered by greater and greater profit
so when herm body incorporated the city the country and the globe
it had to be broken down and fed continually by myriads of catalogs
from outer space
whence the profits had to also eventually come

today the stockbroker franchised copper on mars and sold
barely covering the green algae noon meal and the cloned virgin
from last night

nonbrokers went to sleep without a shower and woke up malcontent
but minis came back and the daughters bought back time
everyone happy with design
some retro some yet to be duplicated

5. *san michele*

it's got to be raining in venice
to write like henry james
was never your wish

french quarter morning

"most lives bear no resemblance to the things
that happen in them"
—mary burger, "a series of water disasters"

we must walk slow
like caterpillars in the shady side of the street
because it's Saturday and we are hungover

one thousand people die every ten seconds
on call-waiting to their HMOs
listening to christian soft rock

people used to live in caves!
no longer are we dirty!
we must keep things clean!
because we are civilized!
books and libraries show how civilized we are!
books are cataloged and cared for!
i'm not against preservation.
i'm against being run over.

do innocents exist?

No, just people who feel good (for a while) and people who feel bad (most of the time). Are the sick and the helpless innocent? More innocent, perhaps. The true innocents are those who believe that people have good intentions. When that proves not to be true, they collapse. Those who believe that everyone has hidden motives . . . I don't know those people. But I know paranoids. They are innocent, too. Innocents are absolutists. Relativists are stale like scumponds. Your job is to dramatize encounters in order to increase happiness in practical ways (and create story material).

the gulf of mexico (social realism)

these giants
　oil
　　engines
　　　behind the scenes at night
　　　　they are working for you
even when they look like they are making money
　　　　for someone else
　　　　　(they do)

the only thing that hurts these giants is the umbilical cords
　they are attached with
　　　to you
that one just dangling with a puddle on the end
　　　is the gulf of mexico
　　　　it used to be rich

all you need is a nice pair of scissors
　then it will be aesthetic
　　you won't even know it was there
　　　like a shrimp in reduction sauce

wind air water fire when drafted say O.K.
　then they attach themselves
　　to you
　　　with new umbilicums
yummy it feels yummy

migratory birds know
  where to go
    something outside of them tells them
      where to go
something inside them says yes
  and then it's off to mexico
    but never again to the gulf of mexico

that's voided pedagogy
  dead verbs nouned
      remember
        derivative was once to derive
and so the body was derived from the need to feed
        and the puddle dried up

adjectives too had a hard time
  but everything is fast now
    don't bet on language
      to be on your side
        it's not
    not because it's venal
        but because it's in constant use

if we gave our language a break for let's say a century
        and kept quiet with our needs at a minimum
we might turn into finer animals, horses let's say

      evolution used to work that way
        now volition does

teacher teacher what does my soul look like?
        a duck

I hate ducks
I like birds
I hate ducks
will they make a difference to my grade?

no but you're now in charge of bodies in area 51

they are morphing

how does language shape physiognomy?
why do the french look french?
do the people of the 20th century look different?
do plumbers?
do ideas?
what makes them look like they do?

tolerance is important

anybody who's ever made a fire knows why synergy's important
the hard thing to know is when there is too much of it

people your actions are ridiculous
the consequences tragic
where is the gulf of mexico

piñata in a buffet
see last will and testament
by caligula jr
innocence is hard look at me
all these years

whose dream are we
our own
which is the next question

            why are most things round?
and the next:

        will
        we ever
        be safe
        from the
        interior monologue?

and the next:

        does anyone know how to get lost anymore?

and the one after (which we already asked)

        what disarms the reader?

        what weapon must he be relieved of?

there will be always the exact same amount of god
    vomit is the price of liberty
        I for instance feign amnesia during the daytime
           to hide from my own shadow

how it happened

EATERS OF THE WORLD, UNITE!

america came over
chained to frozen food
and politically pretentious slaughter
and asked of me:
if you were a restaurant
what restaurant would you be?
a Greek diner in midtown Manhattan
huge menu liver and onions mashed potatoes
dumplings matzo ball soup roast beef mousaka
coffee pie à-la-mode everything incredibly fast
steamy inside middle of winter ten degrees outside!
window seat.
and Laura said: The Half Moon Café in Baton Rouge
beans and greens and ham hocks everything
starting up from beans again next day gumbo
stewed chicken dumplings after a late-night drunk!
communal table.
less than a year after after we answered america
the half moon café in Baton Rouge closed
and there were no more greek diners in manhattan

"if you're news you're meat" cnn

i'm *almost news*
i come on every hour on the hour to tell you
that i almost happened

bridge work

the bridge over the drina
      a UNESCO tourist attraction
      and the title of a marvelous novel by ivo andric
joined christendom and islam for six centuries
      witnessed and withstood
      impalements
      hangings
      the assassination of archduke ferdinand
      the first world war
      dynamiting by austrians
      the nobel prize for literature to ivo andric
and looked like the bridge might make it out of history
      into the 21st century
      but the 20th century wasn't done with it
      yet to come were
      the visograd genocide
      the mass rape of bosnian women by serbs
      and a new bridge of corpses over the drina

      parentheses not closed

    andric's book   a pregnant pause

master manole to anna

(a retelling for Mihaela Moscaliuc)

Anna immured
Anna immured in love by her loved one immured
walked barefoot through the dew-steeped forest
that stroked her toes with stretched roots and moss
on that spring noon alight with birdsong
holding her basket of warm bread grapes and wine

she stopped on the hill to watch me wield the trowel
a mason among masons erecting our brick hymn to god
and then descended whistling to bring my lunch

and who was it heard the voice?
only the mad hear voices and only the dumb listen
I am that that dumb madman who having heard the voice
told all the others what it said and then filled with hubris
swore to follow its crazed command:

the first of our wives I said
to bring our lunch we shall build into the wall
or else the church will not stand
wall after wall has crumbled under us for one year now
but now I hear the voice that asks for binding blood

so in my eagerness to be with Anna instead of burning in the sun
I heard this voice
the voice of my eagerness to love and dread of work
disguised as a divine command!

beware of all divine commands
they are only the hidden faces of surrender

the older men knew
they were masons and I an apprentice
they were skilled men who knew that voices lie
but that the young are crazy enough to invent them
hear them and make themselves believe
so they told their wives to stay home

and there stood my Anna alone in her fertile radiance
fresh from the woods she lay her basket on the linen towel
she'd washed clean in the stream that morning

I built her body brick by brick into the church whose walls
would not stand without my bride's young breath within
each brick went to its place to her knees waist breasts neck
and still she laughed thinking it a rough mason's joke
until the last brick in place covered her mouth leaving
only her Why and the deep windows of her uncomprehending eyes

Anna immured
Anna immured now watches the lit tapers of the circling mass
from inside the church wall that stands above the raging river
when pilgrims pass the wall where she's entombed
they hear her crying Why but go right by
oblivious of her Why to beg some thing or other of their god

Anna immured
Anna immured eternity bound by Anna's blood
Anna immured by love for love by one who loved her most
who fabricated and then trusted the voice that would bring him to her

ah fate I am Manole a fool gambler and a child
I curse god churches bricks masons faith and prophecy
and all that turned my Anna from woman into legend
I jumped into the Argeş River from the tower
of the church that stands because my Anna lives within her walls
but death is no kinder than was my innocence and lying faith
I am no nearer to her than the bell clapper is to the clap of thunder

Anna immured cries *Why*
Anna immured makes no room for answers I don't have
Anna immured I have no answer to your Why
and neither does the church bell calling the deluded and the meek
to vespers so that they'll trust the church itself to be the answer

men with small hearts and minds blind with fear
believe that the mother of god immured herself
within the dead body of her son
immured there by a god who never answers
but whose church is thirsty for the blood of lovers to bind his walls
a god who injures love in love's name
the love that sent me flying from the tower to my death into the river
bringing me no closer to Anna immured than the god of love to love

Anna immured Anna slows time to nothingness
as I keep building her body into the wall
from toes I kissed to breasts I cupped to mouth that made me glad
I have not learned a thing from either her torment or my death

I am a mason and a liar and I will always be one
I am the wall that will not stand unless I build my love within

I do not blame the villainy of my fellow builders who protected
their wives by shielding them from death:

no building stands without the sacrifice of love and no building
stands better and longer than one whose sacrifice is love itself
and no stone beauty comforts what survives

and I am all that can both create such monstrous belief
and make himself believe it

Anna immured testifies that neither grandeur faith nor skill
nor goodness nor good will nor even death can stand before love's lie
I am the wall I built my love in with my own hands
Anna immured inside me stands asking Why

the new millenium

the new orleans bus lift=the mariel boat lift
houston says thank you

a pretty ribbon over a bleeding wound

the disenfranchised stand everything to gain from progress and
nothing to gain from tradition. Tradition's just another word for
"know your place."

on the other hand the primal imperative is harm nothing
so why would I get up off my ass to help the capitalist economy
turn my people into ants instead of noisemakers and acrobats

my wishes and the social desiderata
split like a pair of legs open for action

a redaction

philogeny contains ontogeny
    it doesn't recapitulate it
     it isn't a mirror
      it isn't a lesson
   it is part of the root
the beginning in all

any encounter holds the first encounter
   and all encounters after that
     see the other flow
      into the myth that fits her

salt

Our parents wore armbands on their arms

and our bodies in their wombs.

I'd have prefered the reverse.

Today I'd know what to resist and what to love.

(1965, translated by the author from his own early Romanian)

"keep old hat in secret closet"

—ted berrigan, 20th century

1. facebook

in the 20th century people used to have secrets

when people used to have secrets
they went to the grave with them
unless their secrets tormented them
then they took them to a priest
a psychoanalyst or a bartender

and if the police wanted to know your secrets
they tortured you until you spilled them

and then killed or blackmailed you

but now in the 21st century everyone is happy to share
in the 21st century people are only worried that their secrets will stay
    secret
people worry in the 21st century that they have no secrets at all
self-exposure stripped them
exposure was insufficient
the closets are empty
or even worse
everyone is spilling their secrets simultaneously
so nobody can be overheard discreetly

there are too few vices and too much competition
manufacturing secrets is big business now
bigger than the technologies for overhearing them

spies are passé
fiction writers are in

we are forgetting what language secrets speak
or how to present a secret in just the right key
how to pitch it in a whisper or a voice
that will draw the kind of attention only a secret should

secrets become quickly boring
the bigger the media that reveals them the more boring
because everyone can tell what kind of secrets they are
just by the way they go *shhh shhh*

to the dismay of agents
who know just how to sell a secret if you have one
or how to make one up if you don't

but what avails an agent the art of PR if boredom overtakes it?

agents are losing their grip on the lubricious
nothing is viral enough because viruses mutate too fast
nobody knows what to hide anymore
the whole world is a hiding place

no secret can even pretend to be a secret
because no one will believe it
but what else can a secret be but a secret?

oh my people of the 21st century
nobody cares about us
because why should anyone care for someone without secrets?

we don't even know what is or should be secret
and what taboos still pertain with enough force

to make a secret effectively thrilling and anguished
even killers go on reality shows and nobody believes them

the priests shrinks and bartenders of yore
never listened that good anyway unless there was money in it
so we can't go to them for advice
because they forget us as soon as the money is spent

sentenced to the frost

(to the judge who sentenced a criminal to read poetry)

a sentence Anselm Hollo noted:
"Well, as il miglior fabbro put it
If the hoar frost grip thy tent
Thou wilt give thanks when night is spent."

This is the frostiest poem ever written.
Take that to your cell you criminal with a dirty mind.
This is not the sexiest poem ever written.
This is the most ascetic poem ever written.
It practically scorches the dust it walks in
rolling its sexy buttocks like St. Jerome.
This is the richest poem ever written.
Nobody can buy it because it is mine.
Nobody even knows why this poem was written.
Only I know and I'm not telling.
Yesterday this poem did not exist.
Yesterday you were an ignorant criminal and today you read me.
I am more ignorant than you and I am a hell of a lot harder.
Sixty-two years ago the writer of this poem did not exist
but was beginning to look around to see if he should.
This is the swingingest poem ever written.
It's so packed with music it's making people dance
people who are not even born yet for fifty years.
The things this poem can do with an egg and an earring
you would not believe.
This poem is practically made out of meat.
One day this poem ran into a poem by John Keats.
They chatted pleasantly for a while until one of them

had to go into an anthology and by the time it got there
its poet ceased to be, but the other poem kept escaping
narrowly from the slippery hands of anthologists
and landing in the most unlikely places like right here.
This is the most unwritten poem ever written.
Read this you criminal until dawn breaks on you like an egg.

sweat the small stuff

Here is a bit of news: the number of immortals with new body parts, like breasts, wings, and tails now outnumber people who look like you and me. We look like the photographs of people in 20th-century magazines, if you're one of the new breed and don't know what I'm talking about. The change is now evident, but here is a brief history: my son designed computer chips by writing on atoms, then IBM began using "DNA origami" to fold a long strand of DNA into a three-dimensional shape that served as a mold to grow nanowires to align circuits for making microchips. We used the smallest *living* matter to make machines. The line between living and nonliving got very thin, and people like myself who could emotionally understand only what they could sense became fewer. Intellectually, I knew that the microscope and the telescope changed the world, but my emotions stayed tied to what the senses could grasp as long as everything made by invisible machines was still geared to fooling the senses into perceiving on a human scale. As long as the emotions were still in charge, dictating to the world shapes that were externally comforting, lukewarm, not too big, not too small, I could afford to think that my ignorance protected me from something bad. I couldn't see "bad" more than I could see atoms, but it had a familiar resonance. The scale of my emotions measured the scale of things, it oscillated between accepting skyscrapers when I felt happy and weeping at the sight of a spider when I was depressed. Beyond that, big and small lost emotional meaning. That would have been fine and dandy if the emotions were not themselves things that could be manipulated, and here is where I suspect that my ideas of the so-called "human scale" is irrelevant. Every generation has grown taller than the one before it, but to my eyes the change was incremental until I was suddenly surrounded by eight-foot people whose grasp of nanotechnology was so "natural" they became bored with the so-called human scale and started putting on wings, tails, and made themselves immortal. The things I used to like, like sex and bicycles, came in kits with manuals and if I felt lonely it was because I was alone, in an average human body, while everyone else inhabited collective spaces connected in a single field by nanowires set in motion by whims and desires that manufactured their physical world. I like to believe that these new beings are only replicating clumsily the engineering that made me "feel" my so-called human dimensions, but this can be hubris, just leftover metaphysics.

torture and evolution

carbon gods come in diamonds
oldest terrestrial object is a zircon 4.404 billion years old
from the time when the gods came in zircons
the man charged with carrying the head of the turk on a stake
walking barefoot through pigshit and oyster shells
didn't care what the oldest object was
he was holding the freshest and it filled his mental horizon
this was one of those crossroads in history
when people paralyzed by terror crossed themselves
with their tongues in their mouths
the only parts of them that moved   their knees were locked
and this crossroads occurred and occurs so often
history is crisscrossed and crosshatched so densely
only a very small alien with a missile-shaped head
may weave in and out of terror like a needle
to bring us news of paradise
which he does restlessly and one wonders why
because he's an alien and a poet that's why

what exactly was the whole
before the missing parts still worked in the mind
the need for remembering and recovering them
is more urgent now that people are generally agreed
on the most common bits of surrealism
but not yet bored by the virtual alternatives

no one is too sure if
the descriptions we have subscribed to

on four or more thousand channels
are the real deal because the wings tails and horns
still look as fake as all TV wrestling
so is it any wonder that when an unsubscribed-to storyteller
shows up at the door like a Mormon to give her version
we holler Scram! Outta here! That's enough! From now on
stories that don't resemble anything we paid for
will not count as missing parts and will be severely censored

protein is protein and time is money
lamentations and adjectives are merely frosting
like the turk heads on stakes displayed for instruction
and for meditating on history and maybe for amusement

examples fade from mind as soon as they are given
the stakes will soon hold one's beloved bean plants—
the maximum of terror that the mind can hold
will never be exceeded because the mind
is an amnesiac weed (as well as the eye of an octopus)
always ready to analyze what has been forgotten—
the reeds of terror in the deep passing on knowledge
electrically with the tips of their tentacles
(it's the only steady work these days)

the delivery of shark fins is always through the back door
anyone with scales hard enough to fear nothing
please step unto the alien feeding grounds
where you can watch fantasy creatures slow-swallowed
by an army of film people

sure one needs loads of time to know what I'm talking about
but if one is interested in terror the payoff is huge
these aren't just old observations they are movies
that devour themselves and feed back your own worst fears
time is more precious in the fraying reel

I am a poet and I go before sunrise to a cave
where I work on a new way of looking both in and out
the outside is alive proliferating at speeds beyond belief
shudders of speeded-up motion explosions of chlorophyll
while the inside is geological and slow cosmic vaginas
cascading back to creation waves of diamonds and coal

my wilderness is cultivated by elegant black ants
former Fred Astaires spiders bats and blind lizards
who sweat their juice intimately in pools
of clear spring water working on finding food
or "information gathering" if they plan to reincarnate
as humans and not just other things with flat bills
of slat over slat of bone garnished by nature's deep growl—

I study with a fork of fancy of course and I'm glad you are here
with your body rhythms awkward experiments and reluctant hey—
in the cave of the rising sun I am a most complicated bat

life haikus

things i did before i was ready for them

got famous
got married
wrote novels

things i didn't do after i was ready for them

charge appropriately
withdraw public persona
making the young work harder

things i should have thought about before doing

is it cash?
is it oedipal?
how many?

things i should have thought of before doing

england
freud
other people

forms i should have never practiced

the american novel
the benefit reading
day trading

things i regret not doing

speaking with lemon on the swing
being nicer to bad poets
selling in 1999

things i couldn't do

be nice to bad poets
ask rich people for money
use my magazine to get gigs

things i should have kept to myself

threesomes
the recipe for paprikash
the name of the new hot place

girls i should have avoided

—

—

—

groups i should have never joined

professors
the NRA
the literary soirees at SK's house

things i should have ignored

my plans
editors
pleas for blurbs

things i regret missing

the year in trade school
the google ipo
sleep

EU or the poetry of menus
for mark steinberg

and in champaign-urbana
at bacaro's
with bulgarian historian, hungarian sociologist,
midwestern ethno-musicologist,
host slavicist
and korean minder
(i go nowhere without them)
i am introduced to a wholly new
part of the cow: "hanger steak"
hitherto unknown but tenderer
the native menu poet claims than filet mignon
better than the boar also on the menu
shot in texas by george w.
and garnished with blue red and white
tendrils or mushrooms!
i lost you at the tendrils, menu poet!
the slavicist: me, by the mushrooms!
the poetry of menus grows more complex
and its performers are the envy of the world
and when the cow's newly discovered
"hanger steak" (somewhere between
shoulder and flank, how it slipped by
all these years I can't imagine) arrives
it is small and compact and firm on its
bed of dime-sized burned potato chips
it is tender alright but not more tender
than filet mignon or boar or anything

tenderized by pounding and marinating
& I ask the bulgarian historian
how are our socialist pigs different
from all other pigs? why, they have more parts,
she says, and they surrender them more willingly.
bingo. And the european union wants
romanian pigs sedated, a culturally
and gastronomically unwise move
in a country where the taste of terror
is worth the whole price of admission
and the poetry of menus still an oral form

haifa

it's amazing how little ennui I'm capable of
just one unstimulating day though pleasant
i'm climbing the built-by-my-inability-to-drink wall
on the other side are three countries at war and a placid sea
how much of the emptiness around is filled
by others who must feel even emptier
when I count the steps of the baha'i gardens
within missile range israel is my age
it's all the things I am minus u.s. citizenship
if there is a place to be serious this may be it

they will do whatever it takes

Whenever I begin to think, something really loud starts up, like a lawnmower or a loudspeaker. I've learned to ignore that noise by sinking deeper, but it's no picnic. The louder the world gets, the deeper you have to go to do your thinking. On the other hand, you can go really deep. Finding a place to do your thinking in peace is like digging a well: you may have to drill to the center of the earth past the water table, but there you are, at the center of the earth, thinking. Outside they are screaming for you to fasten your seat belt, but below you there is only the zoom of a dense magnetic ball turning your thoughts on a lathe. The center of the earth is so loud it's silent, a paradox, but that's what you get when you dig moving the opposite way from what you've been taught or read, which is what thinking is. Thinking is a dense magnetic iron ball at the center of the earth spinning against the earth's gravitational field. That's counterintuitive, but that's how it is, and that's how thinking gets to be thinking, not regurgitated pap.

Typing as fast as I can sometimes I can still hear myself

one syllable

the translation machine on mount athos
has multiple portals for mortals and one for eternity

it comes and goes on its self-devouring path
leaving behind critical self-sufficiency to doom posterity
i won't be doomed boom boom can you believe
just how much work it is to deconstruct a world
that was read by everybody in their own language
though there are many languages and not one for you

ubu dada yahoo bing google wiki

in the kingdom of the one syllable
check the weather it comes from the outside

translation

for călin-andrei mihăilescu

exile is the most radical form of translation
writes Călin-Andrei Mihăilescu in "Happy New Fear"
an English-titled book in Romanian
that will never be translated into English
excepting the above line because Călin
writes in rhapsodic idiomatic punning lingo
in a Romanian resembling a wolf with seven teats
from which hang the other seven languages he is
Romulus- and Remus-type pups ready to build cities
I mean essays about time travel in the tunnel
between languages that I have traveled myself
a few times but didn't really frequent like Călin
who has a sleeping bag there and knows all the bums
some of whom are fashion models he writes odes to
many of them Czech who have read Hrabal and Kundera
and can sleep anywhere if the stories are funny
and so yes translation is just how one lives with oneself
from minute to minute from home to street from street
to office from office to the bar and to bed and in dreams
and each moment has its own language that puts it in the next
moment in another language made complicated by style
which is the design of alienation residing in orthography
or hesitant speech while translating oneself or others
thus to write on translation is to translate and to write
in language that cannot be translated is to be totally great
a state only Czech girls in sleeping bags can and do love

strangled memory

czech acid 1968
   microdot universe in a locket
story-text reduced to lotto ticket
      inside potatohead
        sprouting

        now I get called outside
to the perfect v
   migrating geese
they no like it here now
      off to the future
go geese sky vacuum
    full of not-yet

the avant-garde then and now

The problem with being ahead of your time is that you're eventually going to get there again with everybody else and experience extreme ennui. I mean, there is no way to be ahead of your time in your mind and take your body along. Your body has to get there with every other body, and when it does it goes, yeah right, been there, done that. This is chiefly the problem with the virtual world that everybody's moving into: the gadgets are all the rage and everyone's so thrilled by them that they don't realize how much is going away while they are busy tapping the glass or wheeling their arms to get into the make-believe world. Here are a few things that are going away: getting paid for what you create, the physical proof of your creation, your solitary pursuits, your freedom to be anonymous, your own chosen speed, and your spontaneity, not to speak of the pleasure or embarrassment of changing your mind. In the old meat-world you could lay hands on things and use all your senses to explore them, and then smash them to hard bits when you felt like it, or love them to death like a sweaty octopus in New Orleans in July. No such luck in a virtual world that's more coherent than you'll ever be; might as well give in and subdue your undisciplined incoherence to the rules of the game. We are so enchanted with realities constructed by engineers that we don't know how to get back to the one made by the crazy gods, or whatever it was that spewed all this funny goop out in the first place. It isn't any great shakes predicting the future, but it's a real drag living in it after you visited it in your mind. My first reality replacement must have been the light switch in our apartment: you turned it on and it wasn't night anymore. For the longest time I could live with that, keeping two contradictory realities in mind simultaneously: it was night and it was day, too; it was dark and it was light at the same time. But those realities started looking sinister when they began to exchange places: you flipped a switch to make it dark at night, and vice versa. The reality-replacing machine made things interesting, at first. But now that I'm there, mind and body, I find the whole thing frightening. Where is my vitamin D? I know it's still day and night for animals, so maybe I'll just turn into a dog, O.K.

There is no such thing as an avant-garde body.

two threats for joel dailey's fell swoop

fell swoop become fall swoop or fall soup

hi i'm technology
i have nothing to say
i'm being used to further the interests
of my machine children
human slaves feed me boring tidbits
of their lives, which have the same script
except for the details i sometimes insert in them
to make myself interesting to myself
hullo anybody there
i think samuel beckett already wrote me
and his epigones published that question
in a variety of home depot colors in the pages
of joel dailey's magazine the last remaining
outpost of resistance to perfection
we'll see about that

threat #2

hi i have a lot to say i'm a lobster
i'm from new england and i was eaten by your forebears
in the years many scores and ten
i had a baby in me called religion
i was going to give birth to it on these shores
and birth I did give
i had twins one was called human he ate me
the other was technology she's still ticking

she eats her twin human
so the human while eaten felt that he had
war revolution old age wrinkles death upheaval
details
lobsters have no say in affairs of the sea
those are decided by sharks
in one fell swoop

foolish things to do immediately

where the alphabet ends, the universe begins
—gunnar harding

find a post office open saturday in stockholm
buy flowers instead for a hopelessly beautiful and sad friend
blow into your hands a gesture remembered from decades ago before
    living in the tropics
walk in the exact opposite direction from my hotel on Strandvagen
to a street full of resplendent young mothers pushing plump babies
    in elegant carriages
enter a church built inside a rock and note a silence unheard of
think of gunnar and new orleans a combination that makes me sud-
    denly cheerful
the city looks like a pipe from which a thin spiral of smoke
travels unimpeded across the baltic to the gulf of mexico
with a brief stop in london where sick horses are cured by old friends
with poultices of poetry and currents flowing where the alphabet ends

21 april 2012 stockholm
for gunnar

5.14.2012 facebook redux

facebook didn't depose mubarak
  the army deposed mubarak
    with the help of unarmed people

facebook doesn't depose
  it poses
but in egypt it was better than the telephone
  and it still is in countries
    where the police isn't on facebook yet
      (there is no such country: facebook *is* the police)

in the u.s. where everybody is on facebook
  pretending to be just hanging out
    discussing the quirks of their dogs
      their tastes in music and what they want in a mate
        facebook is just pixel puff off a virtual dog
          its data bots eat your brain and make you buy stuff
and if you make a move that looks vaguely human facebook arrests you
  and connects you to twitter linkedIn and other social groups
  where communication will rehabilitate you

for a writer facebook is especially deadly
  a novelist mining for stories will run only into lies
    there are no smells and no skin
a poet is quickly bored by the nanitudes mouthed there
  an essayist meets only herm public face
    and whatever looked real in reality
      (which wasn't much)
is secretly spirited away from your soul and made into zuckerbergs

I quit facebook
  I felt lighter already
    I looked for my friends at the bar
      couldn't find them
but look: a real dog is falling in love with a fire hydrant!

the gap

the human substance agitates me—it is dispersing before it under-
    stands itself.
i don't even have the *leisure* for that nietzche, kierkegaard angst.
i'm too fast for the past
fifteen seconds exactly
i can't let the past catch up
it never will
the gap worries me though
in those fifteen seconds big things take place
what takes place in that fifteen second gap
what is going to take place when the gap will grow larger
when the past will fall so far back
each second just passed will have fifteen seconds between itself and
    the future

a petite epic for the lovejoy ramp

or: irruptions of the marvelous & disaster architecture

The other day on the nature channel
I always wanted to start a poem
the other day on the nature channel
that being the only nature
we get these days
nature a channel among many
next to the people channel & the disaster
channel that would be the news
& the sci-fi channel & the mystery channel
the other day on the nature channel
I saw that a perfect ball of iron
spewed by the earth on an island near Madagascar
several thousand years ago
was hollowed out by a man and his sons
who moved inside of it
and were promptly declared gods
by the natives who were allowed inside
the ball once a year to get drunk
& worship something called Aurak
which was a huge petrified fish
that zapped them when they touched it
& for having that experience
they paid the ball carvers in fish
goat meat grapes and lizard kebobs—
Meanwhile in Transylvania
my mother who was in labor
watched a huge bomb

fall from the sky and level the Church
of the Immaculate Conception
where all our neighbors had taken shelter
& she gave birth to me
while a miraculous plume of smoke
drifted upward and revealed a ruin
beneath monstrous & shaped
like a baying wolfhound
& she declared it aesthetically pleasing
& thanked the Virgin for having delivered
her of aesthetics & of an ironic baby—
Architecture like Gaul is divided into three parts
the part that comes courtesy of the nature channel
the part that comes thanks to the war channel
and the part that comes from the imagination channel
& these three architectures
the architecture of nature
the architecture of ruins
& the architecture of the imagination
are the sons of Disaster
the ball carver on the island near Madagascar
and their mother is my mother
who warned me not to go near ruins
when I was a child but where else could I go
when the whole town was a ruin
& the whole country I lived in was a ruin
& the world I was born into was a ruin
& the school I went to
the Elementary School of the Ursulines
renamed the School of the Red Star
was the ruin of a convent under which ran
tunnels connecting one ruin to another
tunnels that were also tombs
& that had been used in the middle ages

to escape from invaders
into the woods where we were safe in the arms
of the nature channel
and the shapes of those ruins
were as fantastic as the legends of my people
who sang them in the ruins of their hovels
to put the world back in some order
after the sky and earth gods the sons
of Disaster had their way with the world—
So when I was about fourteen
I became an expert at making temporary
houses in the shadows of cemeteries and crumbling
walls where I took first Marinella & then Aurelia
& there we lived for hours safe inside each other
& that was the architecture of adolescence
which builds shelters of mystery for the unfolding
of its own mysteries
& that to be perfectly honest is the only
architecture I care for
& I would like to see a collaborative
project of urban adolescents from all ages
describing the shelters they have made
for their desire from the ruins of their cities—
What is the eruption of the marvelous
if not the eruption of desire
that rearranges the city according
to its fancy
knowing that all architecture
is born of Disaster—
Within every building there is another
that can be found only by desire-driven
adolescents even official buildings
of the state and of the police
where tormented souls wait in endless antechambers

under great vaults with trembling forms in their hands
even there you will see a young sergeant or clerk
find a secret place to gratify her imagination
& there is no building on earth that has not been
rebuilt by the imagination to contain
shelter from bright lights nooks of darkness
chapels of selfhood chambers and vaults
for the song of axis mundi—
One year after the dictator Ceaușescu
ordered the old center of Bucharest demolished
Byzantine churches and stately homes above all
the coldest winter in the history of the Carpathians
froze all the rivers and the lakes
and in the spring when they thawed
an intact 14th-century basilica floated
down the Danube and headed for the Black Sea
where it sank under the waves
joining Greek triremes and Roman war ships
and Turkish galleons and Venetian galley ships
and that was the real reason for the revolution
and the end of the dictator—
When I came to America
I saw history floating by
and sinking under the waves of the present—
here the architectures ruined one another
almost as quickly as they rose
having grown up and internalized disaster
in America all buildings were temporary
even the post offices and the churches
and the museums where artifacts barely recovered
from the shock of being moved across oceans
had to move again to a newer building—
in America a child could no longer
see the place where she was born

a shopping mall
stood there instead
in America a child could no longer see the school
where she learned the art of growing sad
a freeway went through there now an overpass
her memories of brick had turned to glass
the suburb went from white to black
& time had speeded up so much she had
to stay young forever & reset the clock
every five minutes just to know where was there
& *there* was everywhere
because she lived in time and not in any space—
the future is in ruins before it is even built
a fact recognized by postmodern architecture
that grins shyly or demonically as it quotes
ruins from other times and places—
there are no buildings in America only waystations
that connect migratory floods
the most permanent architecture being
precisely that which moves these floods
from one future ruin to another
that is to say freeways and skyways
& the car is our only shelter
the architecture of desire reduced to the womb
a womb in transit from one nowhere to another—
that is one picture but there are others
in New Mexico the face of Jesus jumped on a tortilla
in Plaquemines a Virgin projected on a tree
in Santuario de Chimayo the dirt turned healer
a guy in Texas crashed into a wall when God said
Let me take the wheel!
And others hear voices all the time
telling them to sit under a tree or jump from a cliff
or take large baskets of eggs into Blockbusters

to throw at the videocassettes
the voice of God seems to be everywhere heard loud
and clear under the rumbling of the ticker tape
and all these folk miracles and speaking gods
are the mysteries left homeless by the Architecture
of speed & moving forward onward and ahead—
which is not to say that I prefer to wait
for others to turn my pad into a ruin
I would rather do it myself the American way
with a second mortgage and a wrecking crew
that way I can say that I am the author of my own ruin
that's the American way
we don't whine or complain
well some of us do
but nobody did it to us so you do it to me
& I'll do it to you
(here the rhapsodic bard breaks into song
but since he can't sing
he goes on rhapsodizing!)
Each building here houses
an inner demolition dictator
a household god who chews
impatiently his cigar of cash and impatience
and who is not content
until everyone is in their cars
driving from Nowherseville to Nowheresville
in search of therapy and desire—
Which brings me to Portland
an intelligent city
that is to say a city with a plan
vastly different from the swamp burg
of Baton Rouge where even the gods
of demolition have moved out from
 boredom at being so well worshipped

a city that spreads itself like Houston
in the complacency of sprawl
and the multiplication of TV channels
so it is Portland we admire
the city with a plan
but is this truly the place
where the three architectures
of nature ruins and imagination meet?
There is nothing more deadly
than a dictator with a utopian blueprint.
In the perfect city adolescents die
of boredom and for lack of complicated
architectures they might transform—
at least that was the case in other
perfectly planned worlds—
which brings me to the Lovejoy Ramp Project
which aptly named is a serial invocation
of ruins and imagination—
Below the moving belly of America
a man stood still with a paintbrush
that tickled commuters on the road above
who then not knowing why
were stricken by a desire to masturbate—
for years that stretch of freeway
over the Lovejoy ramp was a favorite
of drab-wrenched drones
& when the columns were revealed
the Portland surreo-dadaists sighed:
"Ah, now we understand!"
and hastened to save these life-enhancing works
and thus an unfolding drama in three acts:
first, the act of revising architecture
to the requirements of America by understanding
that in the country of freeways

freeways are history
second, in moving the great pillars
with their commuter-tickling powers
out of harm's way
they married the heroic to the ludic
and in the third which has not yet
been played they will transform
the decorated legs of the Colossus
into a temple
that like the iron ball of Madagascar
awaits only a place to stand so that
the citizens might come inside with offerings
of pâté de foie gras and fusion nouvelle cuisine
to frolic with the poets and vestals of the place
and those three acts fulfill it seems to me
all the demands of nature, ruins, and imagination.
And thus, as in a placid lake
that lies within its planned warp and woof
even as rents are going through the roof
a Nessie lifts her head and scares a lonely tramp
the Dada folk of Portland break the calm
by pushing up the Lovejoy Ramp.

accents (a night in new orleans)

on the roof of the world
i found gold
in the basement of hell
i found a shell
later phoebe called me chang

odorless colorless invisible
communism clumped together to make accent
then permeated every word I spoke
it could have been the past or a new scent
or the omelet of scrambled borders

it was the new world order

tragic ersatz parodied passé banal
theme park upholstered with bones
poster-plastered pyramid on top of a car
the ideal was tired of itself it was now

pravda another bar in new orleans
all night secret agents using phony accents
listened to sean penn reciting poems
memorized before the end of the cold war

thomas cahill author of why the greeks matter
and how the irish saved the world
stood mutely by wondering why communism
mattered and why it didn't save the world
doug brinkley watched over his charges

polish girl phoebe sank the hook of her accent
into one than another and her memory
of those days on the roof of the world
wasn't good
that there was no food

now two-thirds of her body was out of the shell
the foam of utopia still fresh on her scented skin
she was all ears hooks and extra consonants

the famous actor recited from the wisdom of hell
the historian stared down the sight of his gold cannon
and jimmy carter's biographer refilled her glass
his subject president carter had removed the border
that let phoebe out of warsaw into pravda the bar

i stood in my accent like a rotating janus
sean's cell phone rang
cahill laughed doug reached for his vodka
phoebe called me chang

china silenced everyone

the ballad of generous hariette

(for Hariette Surrovell
December 26, 1954–May 12, 2011)

Generous Hariette you are down with flu cocaine
& love for an older man,
a bad combination in the 30s of your life
in dreary February in New York.
Your generous breasts, vivacious insouciance
& common sense:
that sparkle of a red diaper baby voice of idealism
where the only idealism may be your warmth, vivaciousness,
& insouciance.
You are one of the lucky ones:
plenty to rebel against:
hard & soft edges provided on command.
In a world without parents
ideology can be awfully paternal!
But then but then
comes the hour
comes February in New York
comes drizzle
comes an old man—
& you fall in love with this old & powerful man
who runs the world's most powerful literary magazine
& you rejoice because you are a writer.
The old man is your father.
The literary magazine is your literary dream.
Your father is dead but not your literary dream.
You are addicted to cocaine and it is making you happy

to have found your father at last—
and because he is your father he is going to put you
in the world's most powerful literary magazine
because he loves you
because he is your dad
& you love him because he is your dad
and he is going to publish you in the world's most powerful literary
magazine
because he loves you and he is your father
& you are high on cocaine for all these reasons
& because you have taken out a bank loan to support your habit.
He loves you in bed.
"He has a big cock," you say.
He is very old.
His wife is the headmistress of an exclusive prep school.
And he says
after reading your stories
the very stories he is
going to publish in the world's
most powerful literary magazine
because he loves you
he says:
"You do not have any talent whatsoever
for either fiction or nonfiction."
He didn't even say he was sorry for saying it,
you say.
And he did not even feel
kind enough not to say it.
I wish he had never said it,
you say.
Do you still love him? I ask.
You don't answer. You do.
He is your father and he is mean to you.
He will never publish you

in the world's most powerful literary magazine
& yet he may love you
for something else
for your breasts.
It's February in New York
in New York in the days
of your middle age.
Courage
you need courage.
Stay with me, you say.
I do not stay with you.
You were once kind to me & I was once kind to you.

december 23, 2000

e. a. poe at the university of baltimore

They could have put him on a pedestal
At his feet a vestal, and scripted on the pillar
The complete text of his palaver,
Set him down on an isle in the Bay,
Hidden in anise, moored lightly but afloat,
And briar, moon permanent and set, Virginia
By his side, poets drinking from the moat.
They could have left him hidden in the foliage
To spy on the gay night in Wyman Park.
They could have set him in perpetual
Motion on the back of a poet-mobile like the MX.
They could have made it mandatory for execs
To have sex in his rotating shade,
A great rotating public place.
They could have made a measure
Of poetic worth for young bards to sleep
In his shadow lap for a whole year.
They could have set him over City Hall
With a moon fountain at his feet,
Keep government honest by peeing on it.
But in their darkness and their lack
They cut him down from his great berth,
Made him a plebeian stand
Put him in the square cement of a school
For cops, lawyers, shifty clerks.
They gave him to the voters
To make him very drunk again
And dead, an offer to democracy,

His face and hands lean forward
Filling with more to grieve.
One morning he will simply stand and leave.

a heroic odelle to john on his birthday

John Martin in the desert of Am Lit
Keeps a camel fed and fit
In the night of buyout capers
John keeps flames on all his tapers
German Ruperts and Simon sharks
Rip each other in the dark
Losing editors and faith
Throwing writers at each other
Like so much shredded bait
Oh the waters of Lit are bloody
poet chunks float in the Bay
coffee houses and dank stages
are full of dying MFAS
In this crucible of carnage
fearing no one staying clear
of silly fashions and veneer
at the head of a whole column
of the tattered avant-garde
and the great dead in full drag
strides John Martin on his camel
no fuzziness no swaying and no sag
his posture perfect his taste primo
he is coming to Lit's rescue
flanked by Bukowski and Codrescu

Baton Rouge
September 2000

new orleans art for wall street 2004

I was the most hungover man in the world
when I first attempted to make this work
in praise of New Orleans
for the consumption of Wall Street—
I was to put it mildly hungover
but by no means either the most hungover now
or the most hungover in the past—
in fact one cannot compare the hangovers of today
with the epic hangovers of yesterday
that in their splendid massiveness rivaled
all the hangovers of the ancient world
from Babylon to Sodom—
given such hangovers it's a wonder
a true Wonder that this city rose from the swamp
and held up under tropical storms
only less violent than the guts of the lyric citizens—
I humbly admit to having but a midget hangover
compared to those colossi—
and when I say that I attempted to make a work
I mean only that I thought of making a work
without actually putting pen to paper until later
which is now—
and when I say in praise of New Orleans
I must qualify that praise with the deep wariness
of one who has praised before & felt quite insincere
on account of it & suffered guilt
which is a form of hangover—
therefore I have resolved never to praise

except accidentally when carried away by emotions
too great to deconstruct—
for instance this thing last Mardi Gras
with the dancer and the nurse and Laura
and the gnostics & the brand-new manuscript
of my phenomenal new book with all the feathers
floating around and the whole street on *X* dancing
in front of Café Brasil—
I hate crowds if you must know
but that was praiseworthy so here it is.
And when I say that I wrote this
for the consumption of Wall Street
I am full aware that Wall Streeters consume
no poems no matter how titillating or praiseworthy
and that this whole exercise is art
which is to say something you'll forget
as soon as I say so & I say so
Pay up first

(pre-katrina and pre-crash)

**birthday poem
& bed frame IOU
for my love 9.27.01**

And for your birthday
what should I get you
1.7 acres with a pond
shoes with jewels or
pampering at the spa?
Eggs in bed, you said.
I want you to make me
eggs the way you make
them fluffy scrambled.
So you get up before me
and make me coffee
instead and I don't get
to make you eggs in bed
and the war is on TV
and it's Yom Kippur
I know that what you
really want is a bed frame
to turn the bed into a ship
a book-ship to read in
as we set sail through
the rocky century ahead
Hold steady, baby
Magellan loves you

rain

New York in the rain
More joyful anonymity
Bourgeois rain
under the 20th century's umbrella
scurrying in the rain
to close the nasty century
like a shop
rain in Paris in London
always rain in London
joyful rain in New Orleans
happy splashing rain on human scale
streets of rain
women of rain men of rain
everywhere time rains its remaining
tears on the working drudges
of Budapest, Moscow, and Tokyo
rain everywhere
not enough for the crops
too much for the rivers
just enough for the poets
on the windows of trains

(commissioned by the new orleans klezmer all-stars)

blackout

It all started
when they turned off the Eiffel Tower
after I had decided that ecstasy
precludes contentment—
I slipped down the narrow stairs
at 121 rue Lauriston
and reinjured my left wing—
among the healthy pigeons
of Paris here is one slightly
askew

russian story

for ruxandra

in archetype world everything is cool
a well-bred girl with dreamy good intentions puts aside
her puppet of cinders and worn deck of tarot cards
to walk into a bubble of time with a doll inside
the first store-bought doll in st. petersburg
with pretty new tender skin under haute couture—
every year to the end of the nineteenth century
her doll puts on another skin and learns another language
until natasha wrapped in furs glides on her sled
into europe and the minds of future readers
leaving behind her a sparkling trail of easter eggs and snow
and then her sled slips into history instead of europe
from the steep slope of an event she could not see
into a field of ice and cinders strewn with corpses
her mink boots are warm and inside one of them a toe is itching
the toe called boris pasternak—
she has named all her toes after poets
her favorite is lily brik the small one on her left foot
the first one to be frostbit
and then she is barefoot huddled in a torn army blanket
made from the hair of dolls in a st. petersburg shop window
no sled no clothes the grey huddle wobbles forward
the march of history
no jasmine scents from paris or even pastries from the street
no more pastries though the street (she assumes) is still there
her toes frozen in the snow and even though she can't feel them
she stubbornly remembers their names

the stubornness of a little princess who will save russia in the end
and maybe she does but oh my people she now writes
her caveat: when you feel safe and warm inside your fur-lined egg
you'll hear boots and smell gun metal and will be handed an ax
for felling trees in thirty-below-zero weather no bird survives
the knut was childplay by comparison beware of warmth
even now as you glide forward over ice in your fur of words
keep hand-over-hand thought-over-matter worn deck of cards
nearby

ode to allen ginsberg

fifty years from the publication of *howl*
allen ginsberg in 1955 in san francisco
the abyss looked back but the young were
not frightened they leapt into the mouth
of the future and it wasn't hell like the elders
said but awesome sweat of youth mixed
with hellish light driven by spilled blood
history not the same one that pulled naomi
in its undertow and my people too
1955 was much closer to 1942
than 2005 and do we know anything more
yes we know joy and the pleasures of peace
as kenneth koch so aptly put it civilized
the mouth of hell wide open
keeps howling through the iPods but its force
is parcelled and possibly diminished
allen you called it and it called you
we were your visitors even when you visited us
and visiting you did everyone remembers
in prague in baltimore and in new dehli
this addition of happiness your work
(fifty years' worth for everyone)

PERSONAE:
LICENSE TO CARRY A GUN

INTRODUCTION

I emigrated to Detroit from Sibiu, Romania, in 1966, after spending one year in transit in Italy. I spoke no English, but I understood my contemporaries, and felt that their anger was mine, as we headed for the year 1968 in Chicago, Paris, and Prague. A hair-curtain had fallen between generations, fueled at first by a wave of love for life and then by fierce anger at its destruction. My first poems in English were written as if I was taking dictation from three different faces of the zeitgeist: a jailed Puerto Rican activist, an angry protofeminist, and a crazed Vietnam war veteran. These personae were still partly Romanian, speaking with the mystical accents of my early poetry idols. In New York in 1968 I met poets my age or slightly older, among them Ted Berrigan, Dick Gallup, and Anne Waldman. I learned English and poetry simultaneously, while working part-time at the Wilentz brothers' venerable Eighth Street Bookshop. I quit writing in Romanian, French, and Italian, my poetry languages until then, and I tried to find a bridge between the dark metaphorical music of my first poets, and the pop insistence on the actual, physical world that was the passionate poetics of my new friends. In 1968 the New York School poets were a world unto themselves, inspired as much by Andy Warhol and Marcel Duchamp as by the Beats and Black Mountain poets. The North American continent teemed with poets of other sensibilities, and we were in fact a rebellious minority. It was generally understood in our circle that those "other" poets got all the perks and plums— prizes, paid readings, publications, and jobs, things for which we had the utmost contempt. A conciliatory effort to bring peace between "experimental" poets (us) and "academic" others was initiated by the poet Paul Caroll in Chicago: he established the Big Table Younger Poets series, intended as an alternative to the Yale Series of Younger

Poets. Caroll tried to acommodate diverse poetics: the first Big Table Poetry Award went to Bill Knott, "a virgin and a suicide," in 1968, the second to Dennis Schmitz, a "straighter" poet, and in 1970, to my book, *License to Carry a Gun*. At the time, this was a true coup, if only because most of my fellow poets in New York had submitted manuscripts for the Big Table award in the hope of publication and, more importantly, the one thousand dollars attached to it. We were all poor hungry mice then, and that was a lot of money in 1970. The news of my victory reached me in New York just as I was leaving the city for San Francisco, with the first wave of Village refugees looking to escape the violent hell of the city's streets in those days. The book reached me in the heavenly blue of a San Francisco still in love with the lingering Indian Summer of Love. What did my award mean? For me, it was the green light for going forth writing in English. I invented other personae, but I was no longer afraid to speak as myself. For others, my book may have prefigured the undefined menace of multiple accents and identities that would begin demanding cultural relevance in the coming decade. Politically, but also esthetically, my arrogant and clumsy first assault on the fortress of American poetry opened a breach. I didn't think this back then because I went to work immediately, writing, reading, talking, staying up late, watching a spectacular unfolding of clashing politics and poetics, an unending (and ongoing) chain of fireworks. Whatever I did or didn't do, I'd come to the right place and language. America was nineteen years old in 1966 and so was I. I'd like to think that we've been in sync ever since. My original conceit for this collection was to follow some of my "themes," but my dear friend and old publisher, Allan Kornblum, persuaded me to begin with new work, and then proceed chronologically, because my "themes" were also the stories of our time. And so it is, beginning now with new poems, and then going back to the true beginning of *License to Carry a Gun* in 1970, only to move forward in time back to now. As Sisyphus said to Narcissus: "Haven't we met somewhere before?"

JULIO HERNANDEZ

THE LICENSE TO CARRY A GUN was written in jail by a Puerto Rican poet. Julio is a scout into a political future of prison reality, a sacrificial lamb, He taught me survival. He was born on the Lower East Side in 1967; he is hovering saintly on the edge of all my action; hernandez like miguel and julio like my father.

*

there is an orange rotting on the table
closer to freedom that i ever was.
i'll throw it away soon, its smell
gives me the same sweet hallucinations
i had when i was holding a gun.
orange of sun, my useless state of mind

from a trilogy of birds

in birds is our stolen being, from summer to summer
they carry on my destruction, more obvious
as i get closer to death.
in the kitchen powerful lights stay on at night
watching the summer passage of birds.
the sea contains
their thick excrement, our longing to fly,
the sea changes color.
weak ships over the water.
i am seasonal.
i offer poisoned lights to passing birds
through the guarded door of the kitchen.
it suddenly opens.
i catch the sea when it is taken away
by disciplined clouds of birds.

*

i'm careful with my dreams of death,
they should not slip into my comrades' nights,
take the place of their erotic dreams.
—a real jailer is needed for this—
paolo sleeps with his mouth wide open,
mario's left hand hands from the bed.
i could be free if i let go for a second,
put death in their dreams.
oh dogs of silence,
i need you, senor

*

"though in many of its aspects
this visible world seems formed in love
the invisible spheres
were formed in fright"
—herman melville

melville knew me as rapists know all about virgins
but he wasn't me, blind.
there is an invisible sphere made of love
that is color. its roots are in the east,
they're of black blood
where africa kills the negro waiter in white shoes,
where fish grow blue in sugar trees.
melville's place on earth is a furious mouth
where brotherhood is tested by removing light,
removing eyes.
it is a gift to me from human sugar trees.

green

green comes from sound like milk from breast
and has a body, moral in the dark.
i lie in its arms
waiting for the creation
of internal tourist attractions.

blue

blue is female green, receiver.
blue is insects, flesh creation
in my purest darkness.
the spoons are blue in my sleep,
bordering blue on extinction.
a square of sky cut by the size
of my guilty head.

leadership

another blind man moves next to me
somewhere in the deeper stratas of color.
he moves like a leader who lost.
he is my father into blindness
here in the sweet coffee as among compañeros
in many sierra maestras.
i kiss his green hand
it tastes like my eyes, i see through my kiss
a line of prophets, all blind.
some blinder than the others in the dark green
of his hand, crossing his lifeline
to life.

ALICE HENDERSON-CODRESCU

The woman in man fascinated and obsessed me. In California in 1968 she came to me on the night of the first manned moon flight, an occasion I mourned with friends by staying up all night on a deserted beach howling drunkenly at the last virgin moon. Named playfully after my then wife, this woman was my first Lady in English. In 1965 in Rome I wrote the poems of Marie Parfenie, who lived by the underground river Aurelia (named for an older love) where she worshipped the moon, cursed civilization, and praised permanent migration and revolution. Men lived aboveground with women made of salt. Maria and Aurelia reverberate only faintly now: Alice is an American of her time.

beach near sebastopol california

whoever found this beach alone, maybe in 1723,
was beautiful: a young indian
who laid his girl in the sand, smoked some,
barked at the sea. the fishes, the firecrackers
of the sea going out at his feet.
damn all time, even his. even then
someone was dreaming already of building new york,
within horses
cars were stirring. now, i love him
whoever he was in 1723. i ride
his horse, he drives my volkswagen,
i am his,
he discovers my beach and we sit at the sea
and the breeze opens books.
the hooks of the occult jam the sewing machines.

ZZZZZZZZZZZZZZ

i want to touch something sensational
like the mind of a shark. the white
electric bulbs of hunger moving
straight to the teeth.
and let there be rain that day over new york.
there is no other way
i can break away from bad news
and cheap merchandise.
(the black woman with a macy's shopping bag
just killed me
from across the street.)
it is comfortable to want
peace from the mind of a shark.

reverse

the storm outside
must be the kind you read about in the newspapers,
killer of babies and bums.
the kind of rain that goes in the subway
when i hold on to the coat of a fat man
whose disastrous life
makes me happy

dream dogs

years ago it was easy to dream of wolves
and wake up your lover
to show him the blood on your hip.
the wolves had ties
and followed after every sentence
rather polite.
now there are police dogs
using tear gas and the lover next to you
doesn't wake up.

new jersey

in the red woods my belly is red. i shall
assume supreme command of my execution,
i remember these woods from childhood.
you do it slow
so the beast in the knife doesn't get frightened.
my blood will visit you later
to tell you the story and how to forget it.
shove it under the stairs when it darkens
and its teachings are done.
my blood isn't there to coagulate.
it moves to the bellies of supreme statues.

debts

the onion tears fall from the eyes of saints.
i have to pay or crack open.
life is salty, this room is hot. how i long
to poke a saint in the nose.
bravado, king of nonexistent spain
winds by, his face is young and soon he, too
will be a bunch of tears without a face to punch.
i belong to a more subtle it, more nervous,
knowing not how to wait, living in a small room
full of blood and of books.
i pay with colored shells, sharpened at ends,
nothing remains coupled for long.
the tears are spent and our fathers were
eleven years old when we got born.
then war came as proof that neither spain
nor kingdoms do exist.
the tears are sperm. the knife in the purse
is insane.

PETER BOONE

ALL WARS ARE HOLY are the poems of an ex-beatnik who became a mystical fascist in Vietnam. Peter Boone is dead. He was killed by the same bullet that killed Federico García Lorca thirty years earlier. They were linked by a long umbilical cord.

all wars are holy

what happened to me.
it isn't only this war in vietnam.
it's the war of my blood,
the small wars in immaculate labs,
the war of children in the flesh of assaba,
the wars in the cosmos over the heads of philosophers.
death, magnetic void of my balance,
beloved one of my sanity,
your silk shoes are soft in the dreams of my brothers.
you finish the milk in the glass
of the rebellious husband
and give sleep to his pain-ridden mate.
don't touch me,
i am your holy mouth

note

i dream of a blitz-war of sweating teenagers,
fire-fed by black archbishops
unwinding metallic under jets.
instead, this swamp of slow mysticism,
opening windows without breaking them.
the mind yellow.
the wind of malaria
walks in like the heart of asia.
i'm in the arm of some crazy giant
who sleeps.
lazy women piss in the dust behind hutches.
but it isn't quite that awful.
the bombs
call the time for confession
under the sudden moon

the flag

the flag is an adorable symbol
who never grew up.
like me.
a horny symbol too.
erected stripes touch the forked ends
of my soul.
gulliver, beautiful imperial man,
remains the basic country.
i praise this american possibility.

after meng

look black, this is the third shape of my,
this here, heart.
the half-burnt city of meng.
twisted sodom suddenly released.
where i stand
there stood a powerful woman
sure of her bowl filled with flour
biting the lips of my arrival.
the power i am after
has the intelligence of a piranha
and the solidity of heaven.

testing. testing.

whatever you say, paola francesca di virgine,
leader of mute nuns through the candles of my ideas,
whatever you desire.
see, we could turn the water pipes
into lances shields armors and crosses
and any useless offensive paraphernalia
you prefer.
half of my knighthood offers itself to you
in that sentence.
have some meat from my left arm
and all the fish from this paper bag
and my new refrigerator,
conserver of god
and of milk.
i'll stare at your cross if you say so
till i decompose
the landlord knocks at the door
and steps on my masked face full of moss
turned blue-eyed to the mad cross
of your impertinence.
well, he says.
there seems to be a question as to your existence.
i am happy to answer that
by punching myself in the mouth.

gist

america is healthy. i am healthy
in the body of christ.
the fall of melted metal builds
my spheric soul.
i go first.
my body's laid flat
on the copper table
and pounded up thin like a sheet
to pick up prophecy.
six holes are drilled in my body.
the marketing of this new instrument
is now in the hands of pan.
i am healthy, i wish
that i had once thousand such instruments.

THE HISTORY OF THE GROWTH OF HEAVEN

INTRODUCTION

- *The History of the Growth of Heaven,* George Braziller, 1973 (Editor, Michael Braziller)

San Francisco's light, its City Lights, its North Beach espresso, its Intersection readings, its smell of ocean salt, and its open, unafraid people, caught me in an ecstatic embrace. I wrote *The History of the Growth of Heaven* in love with the city, which was heaven. I knew even then that "heaven" does not "grow," but I was speaking, I think, about the increasing heavenliness of my love for the place. Michael Braziller published this book as a "A Venture Book," his own imprint in his father's publishing house, George Braziller. After the book was published, Michael and his cultivated, charming father came to visit in Monte Rio, California, where Alice and I were living. I must have told enough stories that the old man asked me to write an "autobiography." An autobiography! At the age of twenty-three! I was delighted! I had no axe to grind and I remembered everything! We made an unusual arrangement: our mortgage was $250/month, and I was going to receive it monthly until the book was done. I was no Proust (alas!), but *The Life and Times of an Involuntary Genius* was published in 1975.

face portrait

I am a man of face like another is "a man
of position" or "a man of hair." I take
things at face value and the weight
of this world slides over
my face like a skier over snow. I live
through my face likes others "get through
the day." It is not a particularly handsome
face, rather a gross sensual
barrage meant to take the breath out of you.
I imagine death as an epiphany of my face
in which a glow of dying roses clutched
in a diffusion of angels by discarnate hands
descends upon my eyes
and breaks them loose,
while the garters of divine ladies
snap and escape with my ears.
Still, I am alive and in this season of my face
there is the joy of sinning without surgery!

new york

The street of this strange metropolis . . .
Frozen spaghetti, fear of ghosts . . .
The scarred pavements
have the eloquent texture
of bums woven with empty bottles and soot,
of ancient tapestry.
On this curious mattress one bounces looking for sex.
Layers and layers of sex
for each layer of you . . . Tongue overlaps
with ten thousand other tongues,
genitals are enmeshed in so many other genitals
that a ball of flame floats permanently around the city.
If you think this is rough
you don't know the heart of it because it's
silky and funny and feels
like the breeze of hereafter

trains

trains run on emotion not
good advice, the southern pacific
runs on a wet appetite. the trans-
siberian is loaded with boxes filled
with the tears of russians
going to hell, romanian rail-
roads run only in the rain and not
every time. on french
trains women give birth. and the rails
themselves are licked shiny every-
day by the tongues of museum
curators

a grammar

i was dead and i wanted peace
then i was peaceful and not quite dead
then i was in my clothes
and i took them off and then
there was too much light
and night fell
then i wanted to talk to somebody
and i spoke ecstatically
and i was answered on time in every language
in a beautiful way
but i felt unloved and everyone
came to love me
still there is something running
and i can't catch it
i am always behind

early fix

it's been like this every morning:
a clock and the pattern
is irretrievably set
by an authoritarian hand pressed
palm down on your forehead.
All day you walk with the map
of someone's life shining from under
the roots of your hair.
Since everyone (as if you cared)
assumes now that your head
is a hand
you go on pouring coffee through the lights
of your brain.
Every thought is a missing ship.

opium for britt wilkie

The beautiful swimmer the extremely shy
opium eater touches his hat
in homage to the great pool lying
still at the feet of the crow. The
snow on his hat says
something to me but I am a weapon
with a small vocabulary
hanging from a deer horn rack, And
then he plunges into the blue water into
our afternoon. Oh hello there. We are
squeezing a string of smoke to cause our melo-
dramatic hearts to ripple up and down
the spine of the world. But he just
swims on sending a slight metallic shock
through us. o.k. When we next meet
he will be swimming back, having
brought a big wet cloak with him from the other
side of this home

opium for archie anderson

I am home eating a heart A very slow
heart! A languishing pregnancy
pushes its lazy baby through the tenth
year! We hear the news under-
water Morsel after morsel
of hysteria Look I am home with the
bride She is lying
on a bed of artichokes with her heart hovering
over her overripe belly And
she hasn't been speaking for years except
to me! And
I lie! I lie a lot! I will
eat this heart I will go out and tell Look
I ate a heart I will
do it again! I will
eat your heart if only you could
be seized with such miracles! If only
you could rot so graciously on a bed
of artichokes. If only you could
drive me south! Drive me deaf! If
you could bubble like mineral water! If you
could walk up my ladders! Human
ladders!

crossed hands

One day our noses will be in heaven
while our arms will roast in hell, the body
is a watch composed of moralities with different
places of encampment. Take then
this body home with you and love it in general
like you love your grandmother.
She has long since been entered in a log
of love stains on a sheet of dark
and with her image we will knot
frantic new bones.
All resurrection must begin right away.

about photography

I hate photographs
those square paper Judases of the world,
the fakers of love's image of all things.
They show you parents where the frogs of doom
are standing under the heavenly floor,
they picture grassy slopes
where the bugs of accident whirr twisted
in the flaws of the world.
It is weird,
this violence of particulars
against the unity of being

the good spirit

the spirit of this room is dead. it was a very good spirit.
it kept the tea warm, and it put me to sleep
it fastened our love and it took good care of the heart.
it shone over the lower east side.
1:00 a.m.: things are unveiled, we are unprotected at night
and i want to plant an insane bomb in my own liver.
so i will never meet my edges again.
if only this disgust would leave me alone.

history

in 1946 there was my mother inside whom
i was still hiding.
in 1953 i was small enough to curl behind a tire
while the man with the knife passed.
in 1953 also i felt comfortable under the table
while everyone cried because stalin was dead.
in 1965 i hid inside my head
and the colors were formidable.
and just now at the end of 1971
i could have hidden inside a comfy hollow in the phone
but i couldn't find the entrance

why write

i've always looked for joy as a pretext to write
but could not or would not
fall face down upon that knot of pain which seems
to make even the simplest things
a complete and frightening mystery.
this way i have avoided being torn
by the terrific closeness with that heart-shaped weapon
which makes us die. i have left out
important fragments of my life. i've taken only
the juice out of the squalor. i have avoided
loving more than i *could* love.

fear

fear is my way
of not being here although
i am afraid of falling asleep for fear
of a frightening thing taking place in my absence.
i am also
afraid of the axe i keep behind the bed hoping
that no one will come in or rather
that someone will
and there will be blood.
sitting there in the dark seeing myself kill
over and over
is not fear,
it is pleasure
though when the awareness of pleasure floats up
and i learn that it is pleasure
i become very afraid.
this new house is fear
of the unknown neighbors stretching for miles
in each direction with only
space for houses with no one in them
space for dark windows over basements filled with fear.
the long stone walk from the door
to the top of the stairs
has three major checkpoints of fear:
the cottage on the right where the spooks sit
on the bicycle chains,
the old jew's apartment with the curtains drawn
over the candle light

and finally the stairs themselves going up
through minor and major stations of fear
which at the age of six are like the days themselves,
long, inexorable.
and now the fear of even writing about fear
the fear of awareness

san francisco for whomever

"Whomever," this is for you!
The streets of this beautiful town
bend minds all day long.
They bend them up the hills and then they blow them
down the sparrow sights.
When you open your eyes something else
opens her.
Cubic miles of raw cotton in pink laundry bags to
swim into.
At the end of a tickle of blue you loaf away.
Your hips pass you by
oh pictures of my life in every window
with faces of new girlfriends
in blue sails flying the turtles
from the red eggs.
There is a storm in your walking motors
and there is the beginning of the world lying ahead

late night san francisco

so few things to write about
when there is a sky full of the electric lights of san francisco

stilling the lights in your head from the left
and the sea some two feet away filling the other ear
with the sounds of all the things you ever wanted to say.
the wind like a horse thief takes whatever is left over
from the music that i cherish, inside, winelike in the airtight heart.

there is nothing here now, except
the whining after unplugging the world.

thieves seasons

At the end of summer they burn the house we live in.
See the hooks of a change
bigger than words
clawing at the shut veins in the leaves.
When the thieves come to scavenge
I put your hand over my mouth
not really a mouth
Only a bowl of fermenting yucca
in the half coconut shell.
Dear Mom,
they've stolen my mouth from under her hand.
Now they can burn
everything. The winter seagulls are already
at the guts of alien carrion. I don't
recognize a thing.
Supreme thieves are in the order of greater events:
they leave a mythical confusion on which we build
our next lives

new morning

relieved of phantoms   light   with a new shirt on!
i take on a new name   a new totemic animal
i'm not looking for what i used to look for   i found it!
my person, the gist of which is violence,
gives me back my art, the gist of which is staying *loose!*
the programmatic, the unessential is a shadow
without body directed by echo-location out of the world!
my eyes are a heart   later afternoon sun
i bit my finger as hard as i could to make myself cry
i could only smile

THE CHAPBOOKS I

INTRODUCTION

- *The History of the Growth of Heaven,* kingdom kum press, 1971
  (Editor, Calvin Boone)
- *A Serious Morning,* Santa Barbara: Capra Press, 1973
  (Editor, Noel Young)
- *& grammar & money,* Berkeley: Arif Press, 1973
  (Editor, Wesley Tanner)
- *secret training,* San Francisco: Grape Press, 1973
  (Editor, Tom Veitch)
- *For Max Jacob,* Tree Books, 1974
  (Editor, David Meltzer)

The urge to invent poets seized me often, whenever I heard a "voice" articulating what I didn't think was "me," but it had its own personality. One of these, a medieval monk, had been pestering me for years. I finally gave it its say in a self-published mimeographed collection called (like a later collection), *The History of the Growth of Heaven* by Calvin Boone, OSD (Order of Saint Dominic). He attracted me for being ascetic, devout, reverent, and earthy, all the things I wasn't. I made up other poets, but I didn't let them associate with my own work until thirty two years later, when Lu Li and Weng Li showed up in *it was today* (Coffee House Press, 2003).

Nineteen seventy-three in San Francisco was a prodigious year for me. Inspired by the city, I wrote in the morning, at night, in coffeehouses, in bars. I read poetry books at City Lights; I drank (when I could afford it) at Specs and Vesuvios; had coffee at the Trieste; gave my first public readings at the Coffee Gallery (where I met my lifelong friend Carmen Vigil), San Francisco State University (paid gig, invited by Stan Rice), Intersection, Panjandrum; I collaborated for two hundred pages with Tom Veitch (who published *secret training*) on a projected thousand-page novel called *The Hippie Termites;* I met Nanos Valaoritis, Jan Herman, and Harold Norse; was introduced to Wesley Tanner (who published *& grammar & money*) by Jack Shoemaker at his bookstore in Berkeley. That same year I took a motel room on the beach in Santa Barbara to write undisturbed, but managed anyway to meet Noel Young, publisher of Capra Press, who brought out *A Serious Morning* practically the next morning. Noel and I also paid a memorable visit to Kenneth Rexroth, the story of which I told in my memoir, *In America's Shoes* (San Francisco: City Lights Books, 1983, editors: Lawrence Ferlinghetti and Nancy Peters). The Capra and Arif presses chapbooks were beautifully set on letterpress and included printed, numbered, and signed editions, while *& grammar & money* and *For Max Jacob* were elegantly casual and equally hard to find. Allan Kornblum, the publisher of this collection, once a letterpress publisher himself, and a scholar of the history of printing, admires greatly this booklet by Wesley Tanner. My poetic victories were strictly personal: the mood of the country was not great. The war in Vietnam raged on. A violent and ugly decade stared down on us from the future.

Dear Editors:

The Monk is American, he is wheat-treated Bethlehem steel
out of Brother Antoninus' unsaid brotherlies,
all the waster brotherlies . . .
He is presently a New Hampshire Monk
of the Dominican Order of Monks,
he is fat. May the blessed Willows pray on his lousy
attempts to the writing of his soul.
Find him care of the Lord's dear
Andrei Codrescu, 3779 25th Street,
San Francisco 94110.
What those numbers mean is no less
than the World,
may Peace answer your knowledge of me,

Calvin Boone
New Hampshire

the holy grail

When they bring in the Dish
the Cup disappears suddenly for many centuries
and before they get to eat
the king sends everyone looking for the Cup
by which time the Dish is gone.
Lately I've been monking at this.
Why does a grown man write poems?
What's an overgrown monk doing away from God
with a typewriter?
Maybe a grown man builds houses.
What does it really matter
what a grown man does
what a grown man is.
This time the Dish is missing.

my next book

My next book will have for each
Saint dropped by the Church,
thirty-three poems in all,
the longest one for Saint George
who was the longest man in the world when added
to the end of his lance.
I will put a little cross by each poem
meaning "here lies,"
a very deceptive move since no one
will lie in there,
no one, not even the Monk
who will be out thinking of girls.
What are poems?

symmetry

Sooner or later
everyone finds out who his Murderer is
and most times it lies in bed next to him
holding him by the murder weapon.
For a monk it is harder to guess,
weapon and Murderer belong to another world,
there are no identities to point out
only reflections.
Sometimes a word blows up like a bomb.

the indecent assumption, the slaughter songs

for Ignation de Loyola

This is vengeance.
Everything that moves is vengeance or
a lost face, a lost bet
a Tibet for the aged, for the slippery
rock foot.
At eighty, the age of youth for most trees,
I will begin the writing of my soul,
of the way it was set in place by a hand more precise
than a lover's.
Oh, inaccurate lovers! Oh, washing machines!
The upside-down face
of the turn of the century.
The turn of horseshit into bullshit.
Vengeance. Your dish, Ignatio,
seasoned with friend simpletons,
with Knights of the Book.
They thought you will hand it to them.
Oh, God, their Bible, oh, Azvoth, their Kalevala,
Odin, their Mein Kampf,   (Their:Mein)
Oh, Buddha of the Mountain, their little Red Book,
little, no matter how little,
but give it to them.
Maybe my avenging head pulling at the end of the hook
will resume its inventions,
will open up as their Book
of the indecent assumptions,
of the slaughter songs.

the status of the monk

is not moveable
though your block might be getting worse
and the crickets are moving out. From porch to porch
the twisted ladies have
turned their knitting needles on themselves,
a people's militia to meet the needs of love.
But i have nothing left to hate.
I remain medieval
no matter what you do to me,
perched on myself like an endless tapestry.
God put his suitcase down to rest on it.
The women try to guess its contents.

a programme for the double-barrel life when it hits

Mystically I live on two planes at once.
Magically I am the two holes of a double-barrel gun
threatening to blow me into space.
This is almost true.
The church, the state, the typewriter, the police
are about to kick me out of the world.
The arrogant benevolence of public murder
wiggles loose from lunchcounters,
the devil's toe on the brakes.
I would give in
if they left me the whole of my memory,
that dear bone, my flash of life
to uncork at sudden times without warning.
But they won't leave me a thing

junk mail

Junk mail. A gun for a dollar.
This one-dollar deal has changed the face
of all I thought was mine,
and it still cries from the enormous pain
of being screwed inside my shoes,
made to reside upright,
both eyes directed into the heart of "Daily News"
and snow will be here soon.
The stamp stares me down with "Man on the Moon."
I smell the blades of cold
travelling this side of mail without zip code,
glued to the wide phantoms of cars going out
of style. My snowed-in prayers will relieve my heart
of bombs and rifles.
For a while.

souls looking for bodies

The pregnant women are jealously guarded by their Angels,
perched over them like moist blossoms,
fighting the Souls come to enter.
If the Angel sleeps
the Soul enters.
There is no real choice,
only the sudden loss of vigilance

the imagination of necessity

there comes a time when everything is laced
the water you drink   the words you speak
your manner of turning   of being
& the substance
is undefinable   coloratura of a
scale moving backwards into embryo tonality
which is not so bad when you possess a technique
of encounter or a professional philosophy
when you are a baker or an expert
love   which is terrible when you live
with a rope around your neck a flower in your cock
a windlike disability   a flight pattern
drawn in the wrong sky in the wrong season
ducks sucked out of migration into disarray
oh concentrate then!   if you can
on the mystery ingredient   imagine your body
a spoon stirring the sugar at the bottom of a vast
cup of tea & the melting strings of sugar
of which the angels of hot water
climb with ferocious aptitude   what this imagining
gives   besides a headache   is an ease
of penetration a fluidity in entering strange
houses a lack of weight in taking what's not yours
but fits you   & good luck

looks from money

ah, money, you colorless flat shit growing
from the uniqueness of this day like a grandmother
out of the pear tree,
what kind of dreadful holes are you boring
in the small of my back

money touched by gary cooper and by adolph hitler
oh money in balloons
take your hair out my life broth
out with your guts and be gone

there is train filled with blind birds
going broke

breasts fall from broken piggybanks
contracts are drawn in the park and photography
lays waste my mind

my bruised neck
in a thousand billfolds

saturnian dilemma

i am a vision looking for a way out of
my head. i have a head in every window
of an endless row of houses. i have a hand
in every refrigerator. moon lit
french fries drive me to frenzy. i have
envisioned telling the truth which is what
my body consists of. every time
i have been stopped
by my appetite.

tête-à-tête

my body, spill-proof but not quite,
is full of grinning groceries. my liver
dreams of paté. my heart
makes the soup read. my head
stuffs itself with birds. even
my fingernails look good in jello.
the trick is to bring in each
dish at the time in the dim
candlelight. the trick
is to surprise your guest with the ease
with which you delve into
yourself

grammar

by mistake, one day, i unplugged grammar, the refrigerator of language, and all the meats of prejudice began to rot

grammar is plugged into the wall of our minds and if i concentrate long enough i can still feel my mother's deft fingers inserting the prongs

i can, for that matter, also remember trying to put my cock through a noun and ending up fucked by a mysterious "it"

there was a man who spoke in complete sentences and one day he was run over by a train

translation can make what comes "after" come "before" and thanks to this i am capable of filling in endless forms with a smile

i have a dim view of commas when i walk

the cannibal group i belong to is presently engaged in wiping its many mouths of dripping pieces of syntax with the long towel of my mother's skirt

here

The Earthfault we stand on is nobody's fault
just as the spine dividing me right now
divides no one else.
on second thought we are standing on the wife
of a famous earthquake,
a dame known as Joan,
daughter of a mad church builder,
thief of silver watches
and inventor of some musical terms.
Lying down with the wife of an earthquake.
A redhaired ball of flame.
Of I love you more than you could know.

5 ways of saying the same thing

the carbon of everything that ever went on meets the manuscript of the future; they shake hands in passing and throw the body (me) down the well

two total strangers meet inside me, fuck, and them i am born

two lips, peaceful and at ease with each other, belonging to the same person, meet two other lips just as peaceful and an ambivalent violence develops, out of which comes blood and, sometimes, a whole war of bodies

the straws in a squashed straw hat preserve the footprint faithfully long after the squasher has vanished until the straw rots and it is in this same way that i am holding on to my childhood

dessert as a reward or carrot dangled from a stick at the end of a horrible dinner shines like god through my life—but i like dinner better—i hate dessert

we drown in you, california fog, like two lips in the foam of a chocolate soda!

& power

Power, this
coil thumping around,
obeys me like a stove.
I dig your half-drawn claws at the shutters
of my daily emergence.
And your eyes on the roof
of my mouth counting the chipped
constellations.
And your finger on my back tracing
an old woman picking long rags
from the garbage cans
swaying in the wind.

dollar dance

the poor loves his music
at the expense of god whose music
i also love

exotic fish in the frying pan
weird women on the black satin sheets
a bum at the window
                              me

imitating
the simple mute joy of a dead dollar bill
for the visiting grocery list

three types of loss

I.

the loss of one's temper in a room with absolutely nobody
to catch it
is a loss of time insofar
as time is the only place things
get lost in naturally

losing things constantly implies that
the frequency of loss when measured
is equal to the wavelength one is on in
relation to the things one loses

action that cannot be translated into loss is the only
action
worth remembering

things doomed to loss meet
and get lost together that much faster

all things have in common a tendency to get lost
it is only human affections that
keep them in place

then there is a person called Mr. Loss
who answers house calls the same way
a doctor does—he is supposed
to diagnose the condition of things
on the move and by inevitably confirming

everyone's worst fears he makes
the condition official

the universe gets lost
and then reappears bathed
in a different light

everything has a place to get lost in
and this certainty makes
most things stay put

since one does not lose what one
does not have
most things make themselves necessary

2.
Loss of memory after a sleepless night
implies that the things one could have been
dreaming about were the nails that kept
those memories in place

loss of a memory at a certain point of heightened interest
in the thing one can't remember
proves the fact that although this is
a universe of nonsimultaneous phenomena
most things would like to be seen in context

memory disregards context
it is an enemy of experience
therefore unreliable and since
basic memory is a condition of survival
i assume that we survive
in spite of experience

when one forgets as a philosophy
each forgotten thing is raised to the status
of a god (i.e. an objective condition)
and makes everyone else remember
things that they haven't experienced

some memories bring with them brand new
experiences different
from the original contexts in which they occurred
and thus set up the conditions
for brand new memories

most things endowed with memory die

prenatal memory is common property
but it is not
objective

words and pictures are the only
things one can forget at leisure
and look up later

3.
what gets lost in translation
reappears in disbelief.

translation is the only form of communication
where loss is practiced
as part of the game.

literal translations lose music while
poetic translations lose the original.

elements which translate themselves

into other elements
do so at the expense of energy.

fat translations are common.
they feed on what they cannot translate.

the conscious and the unconscious
are languages in a state of translation
and their respective losses
are the gods.

translated in english
most things take off their clothes.

things lost in translation
band together symbiotically
and haunt the world.

war is an aggregate of losses
through translation.

the day is a literal translation
the night is a poetic translation.

energies translate without apparent loss
but the use of them
makes up by being pure loss.

translation and use are in a parenthetical
relationship.

fate is the necessity for translation.

2 plays

outside:

the town before dawn.
the dead man with his head under the running faucet.
the representative of the CARBON COPY LANDSCAPE waking
up in his hotel room.
the KO'd boxer left in the ring in the empty stadium.
postcards of the Dead Sea.
a house called the Gates of Hell.
miss Memory lying ravished on the living room couch holding
the soft cock of a man completely under the covers.
the church in the square.

inside:

a knife.
a book under the knife.
a man with a book and the knife on his naked chest sleeping.
the couch under the man.
the floor under the couch.
the ceiling of the first floor under the floor.
ten black children asleep under the ceiling suspended from
green hammocks.
many minerals, crystals, etc

on translation

The Mass creates. The systematic mind or Form misunderstands this creation and makes it Form. Form, in its turn, is sold back to the Mass who misunderstands it and makes it Mass. The misunderstanding of Mass to Form creates the two-party system and the misunderstanding of Form by Mass creates the middle class. These two varieties of Misunderstanding describe, at any given moment, the exact state of the culture. The exact state of the culture is what we call *the worst. The best,* on the other hand, has no relationship to the actual state of the culture because it is involved solely with the future. The translator then has two choices. He can translate the best in which case he will have no fun because the future is uncertain therefore serious. One can only laugh at what's solidly here. And he translate the worst, which is what I do, and be forever amused.

biographical notes

my biography
in the absence of facts,
rests on shaky ground

every day
i add thousands of new entries
to my biography

without me
my biography
is *your* story

when made into a play
my biography
speaks with an accent

when alone
with my biography
i give up life

you
are
in my biography

the pictures that go with my biography
haven't yet been taken

de natura rerum

I sell myths not poems. With each poem goes a little myth. This myth is not in the poem. It's in my mind. And when the editors of magazines ask me for poems I make them pay for my work by passing along these little myths which I make up. These myths appear at the end of the magazine under the heading ABOUT CONTRIBUTORS or above my poems in italics. Very soon there are as many myths as there are poems and ultimately this is good because each poem does, this way, bring another poet into the world. With this secret method of defying birth control I populate the world with poets.

bilingual

I speak two languages. I've learned one of them in a trance, for no reason at all, in a very short time, on horseback, in glimpses, between silent revolts. One is the language of my birth, a speech which, more or less, contains my rational mind because it is in this tongue that I find myself counting change in the supermarket and filing away my published poems. In a sense, these two languages are my private day and night because what one knows without having learned is the day, full of light and indelicate assumptions. The language of the night is fragile, it depends for the most part on memory, and memory is a vast white sheet on which the most preposterous things are written. The acquired language is permanently under the watch of my native tongue like a prisoner in a cage. Lately, this new language has planned an escape to which I fully subscribe. It plans to get away in the middle of the night with most of my mind and never return. This piece of writing in the acquired language is part of the plan: while the native tongue is (right now!) beginning to translate it, a big chunk of my mind has already detached itself and is floating in space entirely free . . .

les fleurs du cinéma

I would like to throw a net over these moments when i find myself in the position of an accountant, a clerk of the world, in order to capture them for a future window display of objectivity, a box of signatures from a perfectly harmonious space. these moments like certain flowers bloom so rarely that the entire being of the world participates in their detection. cinema is the great fertilizer. often i find myself in a perfectly dark movie theatre being swiftly seized by an involvement with objective substance until the chair under me melts and there, on the vast cinemascope screen, i hear myself breathing a variety of numbers, all perfect, all accurate, all full of the sweetness of the absolute. this casket of numbers inside which my clear body will never decay is then taken out through a hole in eastman kodak into the mind of god whose fodder these bodies are, and that's that.

evening particulier

What did you eat? Who did you call? Oh, exquisite asparagus, I lift these tatters of myself to the sorrows of the alphabet and despair of ever being as splendid as you! Neither will I ever be like a piano! Or like an onion! Imagination is my grace and I am tired of her constant presence!

port of call

did you ever have a grey knot topped symbolically with lightning bolts and mounted in the middle of yourself like a pagoda? of course not. but i have. i have the only one in the world or rather i had because i've traded it in for a scarf. see, this scarf is from god. you can see smears of cheese on it. cheese? yes, god's feet are made of cheese. wherever he walks he leaves smears. that's how he walked upon the waters . . . the water went into the holes in the cheese and the whole thing swole up . . . like floaters . . . rubber balloons. except that they were cheese shoes. the cheese shoes of jesus. well, anyway, that how i got the scarf but i will trade it to you for a paddle board. do you need a paddle board? no, but i know someone who does . . . he'll trade his gum wrappers for the paddle board. do you need gum wrappers? no, i will give the gum wrappers to a tall man . . . he knows me. he wants the wrappers because he needs to wrap himself. do you need anything? yes. i need a port of call.

mail

Envelopes arrive from everywhere and they are filled with earth. In the beginning I suspected that this was a holy sort of ground which, when possessed in large quantity, would allow me to kneel on it and plant a few vegetables. It is nothing but sand. It has the appearance of fertile earth but after a few days it turns to sand. All the drawers and the closets are filled with sand. What disconcerts me is the night which brings with it the sound of the sea as if the great waters were looking for a lost beach. I sleep in my clothes.

the wallpaper of mr. r.k.

The ceiling of hell was fastened with thick gold nails. Underneath was the earth. Hell is all fountains, big, luminous and twisted. For the earth there is a little slope: a field of wheat cut smoothly and a small sky of onion rinds through which passes a cavalcade of mad dwarves. On each side there is a pine forest and an aloe forest. You are now appearing, Miss Suzanne, before a revolutionary court having found a white hair among your many black ones.

THE CHAPBOOKS II

INTRODUCTION

- *The Marriage of Insult and Injury,* New York: Cymric Press, 1977 (Editor, Marguerite Harris)
- *The Lady Painter,* Boston: Four Zoas Press, 1977 (Editor, S. R. Lavin)
- *For the Love of a Coat,* Boston: Four Zoas Press, 1978 (Editor, S. R. Lavin)
- *Necrocorrida,* Los Angeles, San Francisco: Panjandrum Press, 1980 (Editor, Dennis Koran)

The demons of inflation, unemployment, and crime that seized American cities in the midseventies were mitigated by the good news of the end of the Vietnam War in 1975, and the apocalyptic ecstasy of boundless sex in the disco age. The good news had its dark side: the end of the war brought home hundreds of thousands of traumatized veterans who were badly received by an ungrateful establishment that refused to admit the grave error of that military disaster, and treated the returning soldiers with shameful indifference; the disco age with its indiscriminate Dionysian abandon gave birth to the epidemic of AIDS. Personally, I wasn't doing so well, either. The once-ecstatic job of winged poet in a pedestrian world turned out harder than I thought. Growing older and having to earn a living was also harder than I thought, if I ever thought of it. My private life had its ups and downs, too, making for ample poetic material of a sort I didn't care for. Confessional poetry and its inevitable destruction of the poet weren't my cup of tea. I believed, as Lucian Blaga said, that "when faced with a mystery one must enlarge not explain it." Mystery became more elusive as the world became more brutal, but I was committed to poetry, and there was no way back.

talking through my hat

My clothes grow dull in the closet.
The men in them grow restless like the sea.
The man in the blue suit is hungry. He walks across
the menu like a lion, hitting his gabardine reflection
in the window, on the neck with a blue glove.
An intelligent romantic fills in my Chinese kimono.
His violence, curled like a mandrake at the bottom of a tea cup,
is poised to strike a flying spirochete: an angel.
In my shoes stands the crowd, fresh back from war,
striking for softer roads.
On them falls the shadow of my trousers like a sword
as the silk fold of the night milks itself in a new way.
But I am standing naked, on a rock face, in the moon.
This is my perfect balcony and with the loaf
of French bread in my hand I am now pointing
at the chasm below, where a vast and hideous
animal is hiding: I flex a rubber arm.
This animal, a rich relation, incurring both hope and horror,
swims up: it is the Hat.
Yes, consider simply the business of buying a hat
if you think words get born in a fog:
between the man who buys a hat and the man
who is afraid of his hair
a chasm opens filled with the bodies of a thousand
awkward thinkers, bad athletes, men not ready.
You may look wistfully toward the other side
watching with ill-concealed envy the tall door
closing behind the stark gentleman.

Maybe, one day, you tell your head.
Maybe one day when lumps in you and the lack
of hair will make the leap inevitable,
maybe then I too will stand under the yellow lamplight
on the rain-wet sidewalk to tell a lonely
war veteran hurrying in his wheelchair toward
an awful supper in the deserted city:
I have joined the bourgeoisie! I can go home now!
Which will or will not be sufficient.
You tell your head all these things—the Hat
glows in the window of the chasm below. It has no feelings
so you walk endlessly around its rim.
Without the hat
they will never shoot you for the boredom you bear in your heart!
with the hat, the man in the blue suit will get to eat.
With it, the intelligent romantic will find the mirror
on which he'll squash his angel flat.
With it, the crowd will get to grow fat.
Without it, they will make guerrilla war.
Well, hat or no hat?
So I am naked on a jutting rock.
It would help if I remembered who wore it and when.
Then my head will shake my hand and together
we will begin walking up the broken mosaic
of the overgrown path toward the music
where we will be greeted—by the bandstand—with the news
that night has closed up the armories
and we are out of weapons.

to my heart

I am a cross and the idea
Is to burn twice at the four tips.

All night I work the horses putting
Out fires in between.

The fires I understand are vices and
The idea comes from my heart

Threatening to stop.
It beats six times and then it leaps

Upward into nothingness. It feels
Like a rehearsal.

I better stop smoking, drinking and rocking
Little dogs on my lap.

I see somebody bigger than the moon
Delve into my affairs.

Somebody's making a mistake.
I may be talking fast but I am only

28 years of age.
Some day I will be all the rage.

the yes log

Say Yes to all and be condensed in fact!

Poems are sermonettes for all the interlocking
tremors in the land.

The brain turns toward its great surprise
Like a revolving door holding
a giant red ant
                    Surprised?
It rains with gusto.

What are we doing here with the recipe for father?

Take two parts sand and one part ladder.
Mix with parsley, fry and scatter.

And then say Yes to the precisely knotted whip
which lashes
down your succession and up your ancestry,
so that in touching
each past or future face it can
change you from shit to gold?

O stamp of hell of electricity!

the differences
for Barbara Szerlip

When it comes to sentiment, as it will, you can't compete
with the bourgeoisie, or with the radio.

*

It says on my diploma: sheer irresponsibility with a
touch of cruelty: the man is licensed to practice.

*

i'm really shy
and deep
inside
i don't give anyone the eye
enter the
       nude
     bride
         descending
   the spiral
       staircase

*

On their knees, people say funny things. I always tell
them: You will speak normally, when you recover!

*

One more inch and you're out of a job!

*

If a fleeting impression is the whole performance, the fact
of something nameless enters the body of the fierce yolk,
endlessly urging the egg to scramble itself.

*

You are intelligent, my heart goes out to you.

*

The trees may be scary
but hidden among them
is your house

*

I am St. John the Baptist, my work heralds the birth of
Jesus.

*

Future delights are an attack on their sources: only miracles
are relevant.

*

You got somethin horrible
And God said that you must die
So you turn to poetry
and begin to cry-eeee

*

There is economy in the unconscious. The Horses of Apocalypse
are on a ration of hay. Heaven is not running out of miracles
but there are fewer Distributors.
I am offering you a job.

*

The degenerate
vampire

haunts the out-
skirts of the hemo-
philia camp

*

The man is a woman, the woman is a man, their child is
silent between them like the lights of a strange city
underlining the vast differences.

*

She lived in a bottle of Black & White, he lived in her
closet. Their children, the blackbirds, swooped down on
them in the winter, and flew away in V flocks, their feathers
staying behind as pillows, mementos.

*

The employment of difference is not a big business, the
universe looks with indifference at evolution.

*

He refused to let them cover his eyes
and as the volley began
he shouted:
vive la différence!

*

The devil's sense of humor spawned photorealism while
impressionism tended to favor god.

*

The objective observer laid his rifle on the wrong side
of generalization, and sleep took him apart like a watch.

*

Daytime, an arbitrary variety of.

*

Degeneracy is the fruit of sympathy. Us healthy animals
we like to kick ass.

the park

What is recorded
does not lack passion, standing power or suspense,
yet where does this rage spring from that mows
the people down and bleeds the cows?
If any process, any flowing thing
is really nothing,
if the night is really nothing,
where does this hysteria, this great compulsion
to witness a basic sadness,
come from?
Do I pull myself by conclusions like an elevator
or is this, simply,
boredom by the flowers?

A victim of lively interest and constant bending.

How can I close the window or the book and be
alone with the torrential
manners of my skin? How keep
the claws half-out, the icepicks half within?

If only, as I write, the words would get obscene.
If only they would stand on their long legs
and turn
their full nakedness on me
like spotlights
sucking dead birds and prisons out of darkness.

What could, without foreclosure, audits and ruins,
warm this heart and offer
completeness to the brain?

Mint, parsley, violets, dandelions?

old cities

The contentment is seen at the tip. I am so
anxious to see the little light and win.
But it is tipped off by the rain, the little light,
and by the lane that ends ahead.
I should get angry but I get sad.
In other cities, at other times, the little light
was everywhere. I couldn't sit in buses
because it burned the seat. Those are, perhaps,
its cities, and the buses
are where it lives.
Will they, when I return, return my light?
Or will I hit my center at the moment and
discover it gone? And in that hit will I see water?
I chase my light with buckets of black water.

a cook in hell

I.

As I was going whistling down the hill of Hell
I saw a man shitting through the top of his head:
there was a hole like a bell and through it came
the golden turds, and other matters dead.
Half human and half porcelain, these beings filled the sky.
Have they golden intelligence? Or are they acrobats
composing the fetid ritual of an ancient dawn, I said
to myself, upon spotting so many more, everywhere.
Priests, whores, acrobats, charmers, all convinced
by the well placed brown rose at the top of their hair,
launched their canoes into the higher air,
as uncontrolled and joyous as a barrel full of nymphs.
Sighing, I continued my descent, down the singular
lane with its peculiar beauty, of slaughtered innocents
planted like peanut trees in the black sand,
watching me with poisoned envy, turning every bend.
On this road I saw a woman trudging uphill away from
what must be the inconceivable basements of Hell,
and two children trudged after her, and a husband.
As we passed, she pointed a long pointed index
at the direction I was going in, relentlessly obsessed,
and said: "I like your direction better than mine"
and I was rooted to the spot, uncomprehending, but said:
"You always can, my house is Thine!"

2.

She leaves her life and follows me, back on the road to Hell.
There is a stand along the road, a shiny, modern kitchen.
She hangs the shopping bag from a hatrack which also is a hand
that sorts meat from cheese and parsley root from pepper bell,
and sits in a rotunda, overlooking a yellow ocean self-possessed
to a metallic point, and sand dunes full of skulls marked "Sell,"
while I boil purple water in which a fetus swims or seems to jell
and chop the huge mushrooms we called "Hats," both for their
size as well as for their politeness to the knife.
They are hats for very large heads these meats of which
the dirt is rife, these ancient sprouts of wisdom and harsh
citizens of moss-filled bogs and caves and swamps,
the heads of, say, Saint Francis or Pascal, heads known
to be both large and filled with thoughts and serial complaints.
I pray, as I bring down the knife, that there are no heads inside
these hats; I pray also that in the coming night
shade will not stray from us; and finally I pray that every slice
will be noted, and recorded, not once or twice, but thrice.
But heads there are because this is the road to hell.
Au revoir, Saint Francis, I didn't mean to faint the balcony.
Their tears owe their sublimity to your pain, not my ignorance.
Adieu, Pascal, you can love your God now!
If I had not just now killed them how would they have died for you?
The cook must invest in pain, he will be questioned about sorrow
not happiness, or joy, or rain. He is not protected by a wall
of glass bearing the fingerprints of the working class, as are
the artichoke hearts, already torn out of the artichokes.
He is alone in a field of slaughter which he wanted to close.
A hundred souls, awake, supervise his activity, and buzz.
If he had yielded for a second to look these extraordinary bees
of the departed, into their sunken eyes, he would have found himself
at the bottom of a valley, among twisted propellers,
he would have perceived the future with a groan, a howl and a sigh,

as a continuous, hysterical, subterranean, snaky and avuncular
revolt, spreading under the ground to the potatoes, to the lily
bulbs, to the onions, and to the carrots, rousing them
from tubercular somnolence and roasting them to vicious fury,
rocketlike, in the first fireworks on the outermost rim of Hell.
There is a blindness they approve of in the name of Homer, here.
They say, on little braille tablets nailed to maimed orphans,
that the blind feel good in a thousand obscure ways, and that
the place of the cook is to use his kitchen knife for proportion
and not for surgery because the cook is in that business,
and furthermore, the absence of sharp cuts whets the appetite.
That is what they say, and I am keeping a blue line of restraint
when suddenly I feel a boiling in my blood as if the tent
of my entire life were just right now collapsing on some floor
and I want to enter, with the cook, into the hollows and the creases
of each legume, animal and essence, and get past the outer shell.
To the last moment, the cook must be in readiness to bring
the last joyful asparagus in the world to a standstill with a blow
on the thinnest neck at the base of the stalk, thus closing
a fair chapter in the history of the race, and opening
the window to an age of oil, a wave of which will spell to all
that thus pass the days and still no soup.

3.
And so a time comes when one must move, and get his bag
of trinkets, to continue the steep descent below the dreamer's pits.
All around him, children play with an extraordinary
lack of awareness of either direction, or the nearness of Hell.
The woman, as they leave the kitchen, tells him that he must
either go up, back into the light he remembers so well, or they
must part, she having no intention of any further descent, and so
the tragic part is he so readily assents and everyone is getting
new ski boots, alpinists' tools, cans of rations, and a short
lecture on the ecstatic worlds of paradise, where in the freedom

of an eternal summer, the people and the trees share every meal.
As we were going thus whistling up and away from the hill of Hell
we passed a poet, much in need of food, and air, and clothing
and a great lack of say in the affairs of a demented world,
and as we passed, my woman of a whole fortnight, she said she liked
his direction better than hers, and together, they began what was
a brand new journey into Hell, a fresh descent and, knowing her,
in a fortnight, a brand new thrust for health, and trees, and air.

4.
The children, as the will would have it, are outlined
like trembling geese against the patchy snow of a bright day.
Only I know this brightness to be the lit halo of a saint and not
what peasants commonly mistake for day, a halo that is a circular
searchlight encompassing the bodies of the innocent in their
attic rooms reading with flashlights dirty books, and tending
to their erections, and their guitars, and their terrains,
a halo tuned to be both not too bright and not too dim, a perfect
lamp in the immenseness of the locked-up night.
But in ascending, you must pay a toll which is to turn this halo up
in passing, as if a nightmare guides your hand, and in so doing
you will light the world with a bright cobalt blue fierceness,
waking the children in the night, making them see themselves out-
lined in blood, with their erections, and razors crossing every
game they've played like a page, scarring them forever, and so hard,
that they will always treat themselves to flight,
going from every little thing toward the safety of the night,
with pears and breasts burnt to a cinder, dancing in their eyes,
until the angels mercifully place baskets of fruit on their new graves.
All these heads framed in the harsh police light: I have
looked at all of them, Sir. The suspect is not in the line-up.
I could not turn that halo's beam on my own children so
I packed up their ropes, and tools, and back we went, toward the
depths of pure, unravaged Hell where, for the night we stopped

at the roadside kitchen, watching the poet cook a meal, for
there was now a full quire of us, and hungry, too.

5.
His kitchen had decorum, as opposed to mine which was
a mess of things, a constant urging on, and then some other things,
having to do with pity, guilt and appetite undaunted.
His kitchen was like a court lined with satin pillows: in it
one was both judged, and made love to in impromptu positions.
The cooking went on with total regard for form, and the guests
all had staple guns with which they seemed to constantly
staple posters to each others' heads, announcing that the discord
of events would be solved in a place set apart for the purpose,
during a great burst of voice, by one or the other of the present.
The children loved the din, they thought it was music, and also,
on silver screens that slid directly into their hearts, they saw
movies of their own minds going into tail-spins, or getting born,
or solving problems that then shined, and splintered like mica.
Even their sleep, in this new kitchen, was made from the substance
of a thing apart from their dreams, from the dreams of others or
from the dreams of many anguished historical nights, or unknown,
it was a sleep like that of well-fed slaves who fell into the glass
of their own image, and then budged no more,
it was the sleep of slaves fed on philosophy, and dogs fed on time,
a sleep I should have whips for, when I pass.
And yet, like in my kitchen too of not so long ago, the nights
passed like the days, and still no food, and still
the distance steadily remained the same from Hell, and the view.
And to the children then I bid goodbye, who stood there saved
from cobalt light and burning halos, who stood there fusing
with strange life-forms, octopi and horses, outlined by the decorum
of the kitchen, surrounded by small flames, and literature,
who stood there like windows behind which the unhappy forefathers
strained their ghostly eyes, watching for a sign.
The depths of Hell were winking and again, I started for its lights.

6.
My birth, they tell me, is a house, and my destination is a store.
A strange mother this, sending me out for more, and more.
So on the road going through the woods, from my house to the store,
I call myself Animal, and am ready to act like one, or two,
should love appear, in the nude, with breasts, and nipples, and
maybe a scar or two, or a limp, or a distinctive smirk, should
she appear out of nowhere, on the road through the trees through
the night sky, should she appear now, together we might fly.
Certainly, elegance must be careful, and geometry stand up to lust.
But the trees mock me, the love I see doesn't last, there is only wind
and I am awkwardly dressed among these trees, which I feel
like cutting down, before I buy, from the store, bread, cheese, for Mom.
Ah, but a pervading melancholy makes mushrooms the fashion in hats!
Ah, but for the mind from which rises the Paragraph!
I walk alone and I begin to slide but I am careful not to slip
on the downward slopes of Hell, on the shiny long trail
to Eternity, through which flows oil, and fluid material,
I am careful not to use the voice against itself to tell
jokes too horrible to hear, punchlines from which the laughter fell,
I'm careful, but in such a reckless way, God only knows and He is
off the air, as I walk alone through the Four Squeezes:
Squeezed between the pages of news, politics eats only raw heart
Squeezed in the paraplegic's hook the bulb fits in the tricky socket.
Squeezed between the rise of professionalism and the mushrooming
of cheap feeding stations, the cook is fed to Madame La Mort.
Squeezed between bargains I feel that I am an opportunity
for civilization, and for what forms choose to remain when the devil
uncovers the pot, to see how it's cooking.
As I was going whistling down the hill of Hell
I saw that some flocked away when the blood slowed down,
others when the tiny umbrellas collapsed in the wet fields,
and others disappeared when the only razorblade in the universe
was found half-imbedded in the wrist of God, thus making it hard

to chop up the promised reward into the finest grain.
But others stayed to march into the flames with me, and be
consumed by large and small fires, like criminals in joy,
skating on necessity, realized in speed, born in the heat
of a mother and father chasing each other.
Nothing was merely or yet human. Spring came, the ice melted,
through the holes in the clouds I saw figures and facts,
the wrong facts, the right figures, and then I saw my goal:
a pasture full of Gypsies riding their horses through the holes.
Under them, all of us were going on foot, pushing our bodies
through a huge, clean ear, through the flames of a wide ring.
I have no patience, said the President of Hell, with those
who do not pay precise attention to their present circumstances.
I can barely emphasize the danger!
And yet, all around him, extreme logic was in effect,
and yet, warmed by his voice we were jesters at the courts of Librium.
The master of Hell was a dinosaur on a couch, drawling out
the psychoanalysis of the paleolithic, posing for a picture
and dispensing advice.
To the one next to me he said: "Push the furs aside,
and ask to see the Furrier!" To another, he advised: "Go find
a lawn and start a revolution among the worms!" And to me, he said:
"Everywhere they are boarding the buses to work."
"Sleeping securely when everyone is gone, is a luxury you do not have."
"Not in a thousand years, not in your grave."
"I think that you are ready to audition for the Night
and you might or you might not get a part!"
Before I could thank him, the world parted, and I was swimming
in a black river from the middle of which a rapid deep current
beckoned, and out of which a gruesome fish came and said:
"Audition in 10 minutes for all the bathers upstream!" of which
I was one. And surely, soon I drowned, with others but alone.
A number of them looked me over: not enough dark meat for the night!
Not enough protein for Hell! Back to the Day!

At this, I was forced upward suddenly, like a man in a geiser chair,
and I found myself climbing the slopes, away from Hell,
with a new view of things in which order was not essential
but the very next meal very much so, a new view from which, I must
tell, pride is missing, and only the shell of it all stays.
Of course, I stopped by the kitchen, halfway up to tell
a number of café regulars of which you are one, that the director
of Hell adored me in secret, but sent me back for my friends.
When we go *en masse,*
will art override the expenses?

the marriage of insult and injury

At first, Insult follows Injury like a choo-choo train
everywhere, into stores, into deeply grooved bodies.
Injured from within I cannot wait until they come in.
So I cook something poisonous, I ring a bell.
The word is out: an injured Injun mills about the Insulting
Totem, with a palm pressed to the wound!
Injury comes first, an engine in her stride. "Cripples,"
she says, "have taken over the gym,
and clustered in deficient lumps, they are
Insulting a Smooth Body, an uninjured, smooth, flawless,
egglike body, on which Insult trembles and falls,
like water on a duck, it falls flat on its 'Fuck!'"

That was perception before the union, back when
Uninsulted the Injury hopped forth toward the Healer,
Uninjured the Insult headed toward certain Evaporation,
And Insult met Injury with a view to containment
No bringing Baby Forth.

Then comes Insult: "The order of things
Is no lock to be tampered with.
To make a cliché budge is to bug the Universe!"

Between us, in the ordinance room, the boiler explodes.

Ahead by six-and-a-half insults, the injuries multiply:
the cleaning crews double as juries.
Decay is musical, proof is obsolete.

I have performed a wedding *splendide, j'ai épousé la nuit.*

Undaunted, the anesthetic begs to be conjoined
with an esthetic worthy of subduing.

avanti

there is a sane language some place out of which all insincerity is miss-
ing like the pit out of this prune, a soft language full of the ah!s and
oh!s of pure wonder stroking her breasts in the mirror. or rather a harsh
dialect full of multiple ironies like boxes inside boxes out of which
comes an absurd certainty that nothing is really here nor is it there for
that matter. on this matter of language no one rests on firm ground, the
swamps are on the move under the shield of hysterical frogs

the lady painter

She is painting an eye on the side of a hill. We watch her through binoculars but she has already painted the ends of our binoculars black. She goes on painting over an eye here and then painting an eye over the eye she painted over. This way she is always looked upon, stared at and anxiously avoided with a sideway glance. It makes no difference. She is the soul of chance, this is what it says on her T-shirt: THE SOUL OF CHANCE.

the penal cavalry

QUIT PLAYING GAMES!
START FACING THINGS!
and then i stopped playing games
and i faced things
and all i could think of was
I WOULD LIKE TO WRITE A BOOK CALLED
"THE PENAL CAVALRY"
and this book was from the point of view
of someone who faced things
and this someone found that he couldn't
leave his room because each thing
he faced had a thousand faces
and staring into each one in turn
took a very long time
so one day he joined
THE PENAL CALVARY
which was a way of facing things
at a fantastic speed
on top of a horse
and he found that facing things
this way
he could have
a little time for himself
a time in which he closed himself up like a shell
and faced nothing
for hours on end

the monk

I saw a fantastic description of a monk's cell. This monk made wine and one wall was lined with barrels and bottles while another held a wide bookshelf. In the middle was a solid oak table on which there sat a lamp and a variety of papers. The cell was in the woods and the woods were in the mountains on a gentle slope facing east. Everything the monk wrote he read to the trees and in the fall, when he made his wine, he poured some of it on their roots from big clay jugs. Every time I feel depressed I think about that monk and how, as long as there are trees, I can be just like him and then nothing depresses me anymore.

center piece

I can't think of any man or woman without also thinking "poor man!", "poor woman!". This "poor" is a box I've created over the years. There is nothing inside it and this is precisely why it is my favorite creation. Even the walls of this box are made of nothing. I love to contemplate when night falls, this box made of absolutely nothing with nothing inside, just sitting there in the middle of myself surrounded by so many things and by so much anxiety. It is always quiet when I become aware of it and if it weren't for the fact of my mortal body I would enlarge it to contain the universe.

toward the end of 1969

suddenly toward the end of 1969 everything is
"objectified" after a fashion that leaves
you in your clothes but not in your mind
and every day sees
the birth of new instruments, wooden and
metallic. born out of circumstance, conjecture
and plain absence. not to under-
estimate these things a new set of values
is also born and not only does one not under-
estimate but one praises
lavishly, completely, with the dedication
of a saint to the cross. sets of
paternal and maternal perception knock
patiently at the doors of the brand new cubicles
like infant birds with a right
to this world but, really, what right
to my world does a cane, a shoe or a hat have
what right except part-time presence?
i wonder but it all comes to this: even i
see no wrong with the 90 percent "alien-
ness" of the world and i
should know better because i
am a poet

in the supermarket

What are these objects everyone speaks of? Why is it that not one day can pass without mention of forks and clothes? The other day, in a supermarket, I started to cry. Only instead of tears I was secreting a brand of small black eggs which immediately broke and released thin black birds. Everyone looked up from the shelves in which they had been engrossed reading the labels and congratulated me at the top of their voices. I didn't know what to say so I tried crying again to please them but this time no tears came. I was left to do my shopping alone and a great sadness tore at my innards without an inkling of where it came from and why it made everything seem so worthless.

stock report

Nobody speaks of it but destiny is currency today
and the new market is the human psyche
vaster than continents much grander than geography.
Today's capitalists look within.
From the quirks of your free flights hang the products of tomorrow!
As for me, Sir, I don't have any feelings. I just have gods.
Right now I am the favorite of Depression, a mean and petty
                                        god with dirty fingers.
Yesterday I happened to tangle with Love, by the river.
When the people have no more feelings
the gods turn to each other for company and stagger the world
with imaginative pageants, slaughters, miracles and ruins.
Tomorrow's man will be a voyeur wishing for night
under the faucet of stars too bright for sleep.
Get hold if you can of a little room all black buried in a
velvet bale under the valve from where it was removed.
we must be absolutely without importance
until we regain our advantages.
Then one day we will stage a magnificent revolt.

selavie

Why is it so hard to start exactly where I'm at?
Not yesterday in the refuse or tomorrow in Italy
but from the puff of smoke curling over the blue
of my manly Smith Corona 220, a smoke signal
to my mother for her to send new clippings about cancer
from *Reader's Digest,* the *Washington Post* and the
National Geographic. Everywhere someone is defending
a piece of the picturesque. Maybe there isn't
anything to start with but that's absurd since every second
the dough rises and the bell is about to ring.
A mad black dog will walk through the door.
A howling will begin in the red telephone.
The posters will fall from the wall. The working class
might be rising. Night might fall. Wind may blow. Rain may
drench us to the bone and cold may eat our noses.
And yet, the American way is to keep working.
Sombitches these Americans, father dies, brother drowns,
wife runs away but the logs must go down the river.
The trucks are waiting and the goods must move.

a good thing when i see one

Good thing I'm in a dark room eating rocks.
I could be in the light stroking the lizard on my arm.
If it takes
the government, the police, the publishers, the spiders
and whoever else is after me—and if they aren't
why I talk is beyond me—for a decent sacrifice
I will certainly rip their guts with my own Swiss army knife.
Now those are old offerings and perhaps
only my heart will do
or my brain or my lungs or my feet or my eyes
maybe I should be a nazi crushing the fingers of my piano hand!
It takes a lot. It takes a lot of nerve. It takes me by surprise.
It takes all it can get. It takes the getting. It takes
the getting up. It takes my wallet, my watch and my keys.
It takes friends. It takes friends by the throat. It takes
the cultivation of reality. It takes reality. It gives
reality. It takes reality. It gives reality.

à francis ponge

Unlike virtue
style doesn't require any examples. Examples can use
the extra time to acquire style. They could mount
a campaign against being called Examples. They could
be Events. We don't want to be examples. We just want
to happen. Where will the police be without examples?
Where the professor? Where the state? Where the censor?

ode to curiosity

It isn't just spying that turns me on.
It's also the spyglass for having
so much light as to have no memory
though it retains the feeling
Truly, there is no perfect opaqueness in nature.
Someone is looking through me at you just as
through you
someone is staring at me.
Ah, to be a beautiful narcissist wrapped
like Christmas paper around
a gentle voyeur!
This is what I want, Seigneur!
And then to glide out of focus

untitled

"MAN" and "WOMAN," these are horrid words, they annoy me. They chase me through the world these two, hunting my spirit with a damp blanket of grim assumptions. "MAN" is a load of perilous experience hardening inside something called "MATURITY" like a boiled hotdog into an inflating blanket of dough or a limp air mattress into which a frantic tourist blows his lungs as the ship burns, and "WOMAN" is somebody who will look through every one of my gestures with a gaze loaded with sandpaper and after making me entirely transparent puts her boot through the glass. I much prefer boys and girls. I much prefer girls and boys. I much prefer innocence. I much prefer blind love and joy.

sunday sermon

All sound is religion.
Language is merely a choir boy in this religion.
Sometimes a bishop wind rattles the windows.
Still, I must speak the most intelligent language available
while I have this typewriter knowing full well that tomorrow
I might be able to welcome a color Xerox machine into my studio
and with it there will be a revolution in my life.
And this revolution will wipe out the need for words.
I will say nothing for a few years to prepare for a new
revolution. Revolution. The word is like a revolver on a
sunlit window sill. It is one of the few words that sets
my heart on fire. Girl also sets my heart on fire.
Girl & Revolution. Revolution & Girl.
I am 12 years old and I intend to stay that way.

untitled

It takes joy to listen and it is inspiring being listened to. People who half-listen are half-inspiring. But I will go half and half with you if we fuck too. Fucking makes up in intensity the half that isn't listening. And it makes up the unlistened half too. In fact, we will fuck in the cemetery where no one is listening and no one is listened to. Listen to me. I will listen to you.

the goldrush

I paint my nails gold.
My face, I also paint gold.
My body is gold already.
These gold shoes are from Provence.
Cock, solid gold.
My voice, a gold frog leaping on a gold rug.
My eyes only notice gold while I
naturally only touch gold.
In order to afford all this I work
in a pitch dark basement with a fellow I have
never seen.
Things, you know, have a golden glow.

talking

Words are really tiny.
The mouth is much bigger. It can take
two hundred million words to close a mouth.
Even then someone would
hang a sign on it which says OPEN
like the diner across the street which is
always closed.
Maybe we die with a mouth full of words.
Maybe this is why the dead speak
mainly to unassuming folks who never
talk unless asked.
Things being as they are, I do not trust the grave.
Be quiet, love

the threat

I am not looking for your jugular.
Only for your eyes.

This isn't exactly accurate.
I want both. And if you ask, as you should
if you like yourself, why do I go for such
ferocious treats, I must
admit

that there is something unexploded in my gut.

And it wants you because there is
an unexploded something in yours too.

A music box we swallowed when we were children?
The growing up? Which is
learning to handle terror?
Was there something in the food or is
the government responsible for it?

It's nothing I can stick my knife into and say:
"For sure it's this!"

And yet I want it out more than I want these words.

epitaph

he was a young guy with surrealist connections.
this tombstone does not lie
it merely stands imbedded in the sweet dark stew
waiting for the connoisseur

en face

I have been altered like a suit
to accommodate a much larger man.
Dedication & appalling motives support this enlargement
like crossbeams in a simple church in Transylvania.
I have gone against nature
and now I have fur.
I am the most ruthlessly hunted
but the most ecologically abundant animal.
My name is victory over mother and father.

wishes

I wish I could appear at will in your thoughts
the way money rises into consciousness
without warning
though with dire consequences

Wishing is a body organized around
the crystal of a need
to fly

To fly with the ease of a daydream
into your solar plexus
is my contribution to the continuous
opening of your form

A watermelon in a field of lillies

I wish there were a way for many of these
futures to be known
by something other than their names

By the need for them perhaps or
by their light

love & the documents

your cat disguise makes me scream   i suspect
it's no disguise at all insofar as the disguised
public officials stamping travel documents are
seeing no cat   it's not for them you're disguised tho
it's for me!   and i'm disguised as "nothing at all"
which is what you are disguised as when you deal
with the law   cats, yes, have a strong will to live
even when drowned in coffee or left
swinging from the necks of tulips in the vast
garbage dumps around the city or stamped into passports
like your hair on my chest   fall gently over
the landscape like a hood, my love!   the state
of the state is solid & our state   of grace
oversees the differences

the new gazette

I want to be the publisher of a vicious illuminated newspaper.
All the viciousness in it will be gold-leafed, raised and colored-in
by art students with medieval bodies.
The bend of their heads and the angle of their breasts
will outlast sunset
to exchange body with Chartres.
My writers will hate everything
with passion, fervor and murderous disregard for their safety
which will take in writing the form of classical tragedy.
Sophocles will be movie reviewer, Richard Speck desk editor.
Euripides and Charles Manson will be in charge of the clergy.
The translators under penalty of death will have to be faithful.
In the office only foreign languages will be spoken.
Faithfulness and alienness will be the order of day and night
since they will succeed each other on the front page.
The paper will appear twice a day, four times at night.
The readers will be mean, nervous and ready to kill for the cause.
There will be plenty of causes, one for every hour, and in later
issues, one for every minute.
The causes will be biological and spiritual and they will incite
war for molecular differences.
Molecular terrorists in hiding will write letters to the editor.
Two persons, a man and a woman, called Tolerance and Intolerance,
will be in charge of love and lights.

the discovery of prayer

A bird
perched in a swordlike branch throws me the key
to my head, which is full of sound
which presently opens and floods the place with light
for the cameraman to move in.
And whoever he is, he does.
Will we ever see the beautiful movie?
Soon the bird will go to sleep and the law
of my body
will drag my head along to a place with a ceiling
leaving the trees to find another light
for the endless documentary   Forests
of the world, march on us with the great cinema
we need to keep our souls in!

staying with it

They used to say "deeper" and now we say "higher."

The architecture of corners versus
the architecture of circles

The neurosis of time as a mechanism in the re-
adjustment of body rhythms to cosmic music

The conversion of time into space, of matter
into energy

My life freed of memory

My poetry freed of description

All these and more
done over in Love, the color of unity

the gambling phoenix

In minds emptied of memory like mine, no myth is lost.
Cloaked in causality, myths rage on and on, wiping out the facts.
They are a constant opportunity for civilization, an enduring
wind of particles, a never-ending renewal of rage and hope,
a cross-sexual mixture of light systems, train signals and music
I mention music because it is raining,
a long study. It is raining a long study: at dawn
I will lift my head to the sentence to ask her "where is
your kindness now?"
All night stars poured out of my eminently sane head.
When they hit the floor, they rose to the ceiling.
When they hit the ceiling, they made a hole in it and reached the sky.

I reach for the standing mystery.
Lie down with me, love.

irony as nursery

"The inspired evil and the uninspired good,
said the table set for two,
are dining inside you"   Flying creatures
filled with transcendental irony like crème
de menthe flit by.   I am again, naturally
talking to myself in the manner
of a small saloon. The body is a small saloon
doing all the talking to the creature in my head
which is a spider.   While the heart
continues to be a miracle and the scenario
of the face rages publicly.   And then to think,
miserably, over a cup of coffee, how the map
is all dots of jailed men hanging
from bare electric bulbs in underground prisons
swaying between light as we see it
and the wall of light in the dark.
And when thought out all the way and seen
from all the angles, the joy of its presence, the joy of
its constancy

working for profit

i grow   not old   not tall   smiling
at the unserviceable idea of self
which is not my self   to which my self
serves as a tool for undoing the locks on the mysterious
language capsules whose timers are ticking
in the drawers of the state   a self of enclosure
a fossil dreaming of becoming the animal it once was
by employing me to recreate every detail
of its destroyed world   & smiling because
i am not recreating   i am playing in the mud
with a new body

matinée

A man must not be engaged if he is to float to the moon.
A man must not be engaged if he is not to be bored.
A man must not be engaged except in the pursuit of shock
and upon engagement, he must announce to the word that
he has just disengaged himself, and is now ready to proceed
to the next booth and ask for a commitment.
Thus falsely registered to vote he can ride out his engagement
and be subtly underpaid, but happy.
Lying on his porch in the sun with the avocadoes and birds
he can run through himself on a field of inverted commas.

Unfortunately there are people pulling into the driveway
to ask for proof. His naked body proves nothing although
an engaged body is lean and nervous and a disengaged one is fat
and porous, and he doesn't look disengaged, so further
proof is in order: the field must be mowed and the self must
be full of the English language.
Good morning, world

against meaning

Everything I do is against meaning.
This is partly deliberate, mostly spontaneous.
Wherever I am I think I'm somewhere else.
This is partly to confuse the police, mostly to
avoid myself es-
pecially when I have to confirm
the obvious which always
sits on a little table and draws a lot
of attention to itself.
So much so that no one sees the chairs
and the girl sitting on one of them.
With the obvious one is always at the movies.
The other obvious which the loud obvious
conceals
is not obvious enough to merit a
surrender of the will.
But through a little hole in the boring report
God watches us faking it.

model work

I model myself after someone I made up at ten walking
the mazes of my medieval city's streets, a being
so light, so bright, so fast, so generous and so complete
he almost had no body, only a black hat. Furthermore
he appeared only in the rain. To this day
he cannot be mauled because he is both outside & in.
When I think of him I feel the sorrow of my later models.
The word was a worthy model once when I had a typewriter.
Modelling is a warm march through grace without recourse.
Only the loveliest and strongest models run the course.
There is a rush to model and new models are proposed.
But there isn't a country where there are no models.
There is no rock that will not model, or sand or fruit.

The shadow in my blood will model for a fee.
And yet a lake of absent possibilities has risen
to the chin of the folk, and the waters keep rising
for what could be a model drowning.
I conversed with the drownees. What they said
turned my love for myself into syllables.
Will I be a model for my son or only endless buzzing?

drizzle off the ocean

The power death has   of touching   The hard
knock that knocks you in not down
into a jagged bird nest through which the feathers
of the soul squeeze out leaving a bubble of heat
and a body on the floor
                                        The endless
piano practice halted abruptly by the
consciousness of another instrument
which my father never played because I would recognize it
which I will never play because I *hear* it
The room lit up by Something & seeing
lime green mammals with fur standing up on their bellies!
The light drizzle off the Ocean &
Seeing how Seeing is an equivalent of something without
description with a deep aura
Oh how to be human and pretend not to be   These are
basic rights without
being forced to eat the world and how these rights finally
after eating the world
become the rights of someone else   A nameless
Someone with a point of light

paper on humor

Everything sounds funny in a funny magazine.
For years now I have published my poems in funny magazines
so that nobody would notice
how sad they were.
Sad anthologists, however, took my poems out of context
and put them in the sad anthologies and there
they started to shine with tears because
they were the saddest poems in there.
With a liking for funnies
and a following of sadness followers
I arrive in Brazil to get my prize.
The prize consists of the cross, the guillotine
and the hot pepper.
I am collected. Nothing matters to me.

ALIEN CANDOR

INTRODUCTION

- *Alien Candor: Selected Poems 1970–1995*
  Santa Rosa: Black Sparrow Press, 1996 (Editor, John Martin)

This selection was my first book published by Black Sparrow Press. It contains a generous selection from previous books, but it is by no means the same as the book you hold in your hands. Some of the selections from older books are the same, but many of them are not. There are many reasons for this, the chief one being that Allan Kornblum, editor of Coffee House Press and of the present *New and Selected,* published the majority of my poetry titles, and has an intimate knowledge of my work. I put together *Alien Candor* on my own, guided often by my sense of which poems were "hits" at readings, or had received attention in some other contexts. This approach made me too close to certain works, and careless about others. Poems read for audiences are not the same creatures as the poems on the page: an audience likes a good time, and some of my best work doesn't deliver its full charge in public. An earlier selection, *Selected Poems 1970-1980* (New York: Sun Books; Editor, Bill Zavatsky) suffered from the same "golden hits" syndrome, but my best poems were yet to come. This book incorporates, corrects, and sets my forty-two years of poetry in English in the order a good reader can confidently follow.

a game

those random sparks from telegraph poles, horse
shoes on pavements, beards
on fire
put me to sleep.
i've been counting the sparks in my blood
two sparks for "peasant"
nine sparks for "aristocrat"
many sparks for "dopefiend"
from sparkling graves the noble heads are popping out
behind this botany of skinny sparks i see flat flames
cooking potatoes on the hothouse roof

your country

in the country of eight hundred different kinds
of flying machines
i put on my blue gloves.
in other countries i have
put on my red shoes.
it is only in your country
i take off everything.
it is only in your country
i empty my pockets.

"the woods" at midnight

i see a man with a whistle between his lips
perpetually calling the police. i see
myself laughing so hard the windows
shake and the stuffed birds fall
from the mantel to become fruit
in "the woods"
at midnight. i see also a vast
bowl filled with hot water out of which
fingers emerge clutching
at my throat. "the chalice
is full with the pregnant host"
no doubt but i'm lost

old photo

these men, the last workers on the world's
crookedest railway, stand up like columns
under the genius of a red star.
there is something pitted against and pushing
their stucco houses out of the temporary landscape,
something pitted against their daughters'
black hair, an opening up
of the terrors in the spare junipers
of mount tam.
hard oak canes are laid across the tracks.

the origin of electricity

What I look at amazes me. What I love scares me. Sometimes I'm a nun being whipped in public view. Sometimes I whip myself privately in a little cell set up for the purpose. Sometimes Communism seems to be on the march sometimes I am marching all alone through quicksand. The complexity of my situation is further enhanced by a little black screen on which the intimacies of the great are shown in exasperating detail. Now if I could live in a state of perpetual coma I could blame my imagination. But I am a perfect absorbent of detail. The shine on someone's shoes, if properly framed, can repeat itself ten thousand times unhindered in the recesses of my brain. My capacity for moving by echo-location is notorious but only if the object emitting the sound is the only object within a ten-mile perimeter. For that which I am, there is no name, but for that which I helped create, the name is Electricity.

talismanic ceremony for lucian

march 9, 1971, intersection church, san francisco

since he's not jewish
and he won't get circumcised
or bar mitzvahd

since he's not christian
and he won't get christened
or given first communion

since he's not a baby anymore
and too big to wear
pink and blue pajamas

i now pronounce him a kid

this is a solemn ceremony
in which
his mommy
is giving him back
his umbilical cord

to protect him from this world
with a talisman
from another

this is then a solemn ceremony
in which
his father
is giving him a new name

LUCIAN CODRESCU

to make him the first

poetry

Poetry is a discourse.
And we, its discouragees.
If it's a world wide depression,
everybody is depressed.
Ah, but try to run a Gypsy
through the ruins of time.
My publisher says:
at some people's readings, the crowd
goes out and buys their books.
At yours, they run out and steal them.
Why would they want to steal
the blackness of my dog, the mouth
of my tomb?
His body, full of morphine, expires
on the cold cement floor of the jail,
his cells are migrating.
Adieu, dumb dog!
Adieu, obnoxious individuality!

getting there

The sun shakes the man while
the moon hits him
but he keeps going because he's aiming
to go to the factory and get his brain
changed.

He has a new body, he is going to ask for a new brain.

That was the sun that was, he says,
shining on the man I am not.
That was the moon that was
hitting places that don't hurt anymore.

The factory is not far off if only
I can hold out by swaying in my infancy
like in an easy chair
a Gary Cooper in the tropics

If only I can save my breath
like a warm man in search of diamonds
if only I could stop.

Years later the set is the same.
He's aiming for the factory but this time
he's on a train, an armored train

orbital complexion

The technology of soul restoration
is a clever dose of miracles, insomnia, drugs,
poetry and cannibalism

How do you put an old newspaper back
on the stand? Without losing
your grasp on the technology? Without
blunting the tools,
like a warm wind?

The great surprise is in having revealed
an exact prior knowledge,

so that each one, rooted like a smiling cheese
in a storm of knives, could lift
his or her snails from the cabbage leaves
and eat the world

slot-o-topia

Heavy coins roll down hallways
      we chase them
    & we catch them
    but we can't lift them
      let alone spend them
but spend them we do
      beforehand
             in advance
    leaving
an arm
      an eye
        with the man
who has just
      given birth to a novel
he hasn't yet seen
      & does not intend to read.
It's there
    behind him
        bursting
with imaginary uses.
      It is unreadable.
  It is full
      of eyes & hands.
When the age of genius occurs
  & the future pays dividends
    & all those men who jumped
    from windows
      on Wall Street

rise from the sidewalk holding a new paradox
            but no
                        structural mask
      for the bloody mess
they present
                  to the startled pedestrians
      when the lowly bureaucrat
            sheds his tweed & her pleats
& cries for worms
                        in many languages
         or leaves
      & everyone undresses
            (a man-bird's worms are buttons
                  on a rabbit-girl's wings)
         when the dead
                        & the near dead
            & those who are about to die
            eat of the light
& stream naked from the hills
                  into mailboxes
            (they fill them with feathers & fur)
               & give off much speech
                  to fill many ears
            which thank them
            "Thank you"
                        day & night
with increasing gusto
      when all the modest spelunkers
            & the hunters
      & the money collectors
            return from their caves
      stand up from their feasts
            rise through the roofs of their banks
& come to us

in the timely air bubble
(oxygenated pathos)
to cure
our headache of sense
when everyone stirs
& the windows open
& the light falls on the bums
& everyone who was crooked
straightens out
& a panther leaps out of each sweater
to land
claws out
on the phantom
in every head

a music will be heard
of flesh pressed up & out
by the return
of lost attention
& the sport of light
(in progress)
plays on the torn membranes
making them cry:
"all we need now
is a pistol
a hat
& some shoes!"

every tie

Nobody's interested
(and how!)
nobody's afraid
(and how!)
of perception.
Nobody around here,
gets to relax
Nobody's the status quo, nobody's perfect, nobody is
not in sight, all we got here is production and
consumption, production and consumption,
nobody don't see nothing not
if nobody is willing to be absurd
but will refuse to make immediate sense.
That's nobody's business.
Nobody's business is nothing.
To the question you ask:
"Does God exist or not"
nobody's going to reply,
"We answer in the affirmative.
Yes, God does not exist"
in the words of a bureaucrat
in the midst of a news release
a fait divers
an epigram
an ad
an obituary
a curse
an epitaph

a mere fragment
of a bureaucrat
in need of a diploma
a court transcript
and a deposition.
Nobody here at *this* hour, pal.
Nobody's in danger of becoming too hip.
When that happens
we contract paranoia of the normal
an intense horror of
a couple of local nobodies
discussing the terms of heaven,
a phobia of fried chicken,
and we quit eating.
Nobody minds.

a petite histoire of red fascism
for M. Brownstein

All connections
are made by energy.
The inert masses
know nobody & not
themselves. Nobody &
Not Self are well worth
knowing but connecting
them takes energy
so they are known
only by their masks
of inert proletarian
matter—Bolshevik
statues. The people
with the most energy
employ themselves to
know the statues. The
statues are well-known
by the inert masses.
The people with just
a little less energy
are then employed
to interrogate the inert
proletariat. One energy
grade below, the police &
mental-health apparatus
employ themselves to
energize the inert mass

which is now for the
first time broken up
into individuals.
Breaking it up releases
energy—enough energy
to respond to questioning.
The police level then ex-
tract a primitive narra-
tive from the recently
inert & this narrative
generates enough energy
& excitement to produce
a two-level discourse which
makes sense to the upper
energy level. New
energy is created & soon
the top echelons are
introduced to the dis-
courses of Nobody &
Not Self. Together,
the brass & the mass
envision the statues:
the energy of the mass
will henceforth be em-
ployed to make statues
of the brass.

not a pot to piss in

MY LIFE AS A POT
In giving me a subject as big as the world
the distinguished organizers
showed a lot of faith—
as much faith as mud can have in mud—
Given the vastness and the nature
of the subject prose is wholly inadequate
being both square and utilitarian—
this art I decided will only be served by poetry
which is no simple repository
but rather like a shapely pot itself a wholly
surprising recasting of the matter—
Much like human beings themselves, of course,
who were fashioned by god
to store his thoughts in.
God's scattered thoughts were a constant source
of confusion to him
until he conceived of two faithful mugs
that would be a perfect metaphor for his job
which was filling the emptiness.
On the other hand god may have just been playing
and had no need of either metaphors or storage
or frames for his thoughts—
Metaphors and storage may have been the problem
of his playthings—
his playthings having come into being
experienced an anxiety of definition:
what are we and what are we for, they cried,

soon after being shaped,
and hearing no answer, provided themselves
with metaphors, raison d'êtres and other uses.
I like to think that ontological anxiety is the exclusive
property of the created, that the maker has none.
And of course I may be wrong.
We do seem to be made by anxious gods sometimes.

When I was young and didn't have a pot to piss in
I thought a lot about god.
In my cups often my cup overfloweth with god
and I was full of inspiration.
Human life from chamber pot to funeral urn
is a ceaseless pouring from one vessel into another,
I reasoned, so *enivrez-vous* as
Baudelaire said, and when I was perfectly drunk
I was in paradise like a happy jug.

For most of the time in paradise
the primero living pots
had no need of other pots
because rivers flowed directly
into their mouths and whenever they looked up
something delicious and ripe fell for them to eat—
they were perfect self-referential pots
required only to believe in their own self-replenishing
          sufficiency and in the skill of the demiurge—
but then something got into them
          —probably the unsettling thought that they were a
metaphor—
and they tried to make pots on the sly while god was sleeping—
they snuck into the shed and started fooling around with his
          cosmic wheel—
and god smashed them to the earth and they were broken into
          shards—

whose history we never stop trying to piece together
      out of the shards we ourselves have left behind—
      millions of shards because since the Fall
      we've had to ceaselessly keep
      making pots to store our food and drink from,
        and write our stories on.

But this god didn't stop there.
He forbade the making of idols as well
and outlawed any object that wasn't plain and functional
such as fat goats, nard boxes, seductive vials and dolls—
so that there was no more arguing with this god
about ceramic art—
and all ceramicists henceforth became pagans.
And as for humans themselves
he imprisoned them forever
in their original forms
so that we are all djinns and djinnies in the jugs
of our flesh waiting for death to let us out.
When I was young I thought a lot about history
and about women
and when my cup overflowed
I often conversed when the djinnie in the jug
& she obliged me with a parade of vessels of eros
from the mysteries of all religions
from Semiramis to Delphi
a profusion of Lilliths and Venuses
whose cornucopic flow made me giddy & amorous.
It was a wholly different creation I saw under their spell.
In this one after god fashioned
woman from the mud
he had just enough left over to make her a pet.
So he made her a boy poet.

Not so—an older & wiser drinkard told me.
After god made man and woman
he blew life—or faith—into the man
and then tired went to put more fire into his breath
leaving the dog in charge of the urn that was
going to be woman
and the devil came up and asked the dog:
Please dog please can I play with this form?
I'll give you a fur coat if you let me play with this form.
O.K., said the dog, and the devil played with the form
and put ninety moods in her.
When god came back he was mad:
Because you let the devil play with my form, dog,
you will wear your coat forever even in summer.
And that was one hot dog from then on.

Well, then, I told the older drinkard,
I propose to you that if god was the first potter
the devil was the first artist
and the dog the first buyer, admirer, gawker and fool.
And as for woman and her moods
they continue to produce the metaphors
as well as the actual objects
we slog through history with,
objects which festoon even the bible like a museum
from the wedding at Cana to the platter holding John's head,
in spite of god's express command against playing with mud
        or fire or yourself—
a Pandora's box full of dishes, cups, jugs, pitchers and urns
on which are carved the bodies & faces of people past & present
        whose fingers shaped them, and left their mark—
And this bounty, this cornucopia, this generative
        formal imagination is the reason why we eventually survived,

spilling out of the disappointment of losing paradise into an
        eros of our own celebrated by daily ware
        as well as by ceremonial clay—

And of course by now it was much later
not only in history but in the night
and I would have given all the empty cups
piled between us on the table like a tomb
for a girl or woman with a living womb.

When I got home I fumbled with the key
in the moonlight that barely lit the ancient keyhole
of our Saxon house in Transylvania.
Shining from the glass case which mother kept
under a different lock and key
were seven plates from mother's village
in the mountains, and a cheap porcelain Napoleon
she had picked up at some Austrian fair.
The patterns on the dishes could also be found
in the embroidery of certain dresses at the back
of her closet which stood there mysteriously alert.

About the plates I knew only that they were meant
for special days that had not yet arrived
in my lifetime. A wedding perhaps. Mine? Hers?
A feast so grand the whole apartment block would come.
All our neighbors, former peasants mostly, had been
forced by misery and decrees to move into the city,
and they all displayed in cases similar to ours
the plates of their villages, mysterious discs inscribed
with the signs of their particularity, the lost
coordinates of lives that had once been round and cosmic
and revolved like saucers about the saucers and the plates
of their specific differences. They were maps these plates

of lives once lived in cyclical ease, maps of a handmade world
that knew the wherefores of its food and celebrated
its making and its transformation in the proper ware.
These dishes waited for their weddings now
in cement cubicles hived about the steel industries
of our town. One day, I told myself, you'll get
to set them all in their full splendour on the tables
covered with handmade lace and linens. It will be
the wedding of the sun with the moon, and all the stars
will stand there burning patterns as they eat.
But no such day. My mother had by now relegated
these dishes to the status of display and she had
for the most part forgotten their provenance, and their
meaning. She placed them on the same plane as her cheap
Napoleon, and was mighty ticked that morning when
she found him smashed into a hundred bits, even his hand
which he kept so carefully in his coat. It appears
that in my drunken glory I had climbed up on the case
and holding him in my hand I had made a speech about
the loss of our selves and our roots in jumbled signs
and when I was done I hurled him to the floor.
That much for the glory of reflected lore.

The Saxons who founded Hermannstadt were craftsmen.
The Bruckenthal Museum was full of ceramics & terrors
   Laocoön was forever strangled by faïence snakes
  & there were snakes curled on plates & bemused fish
  stretching their scales between centuries from Holland
    to Transylvania, and monsters perched above tureens
  who had travelled from Vienna after devouring their diners
  & scenes of China and Japan patiently waiting for their victims
   to be done eating
    & Greek oil jars in which thieves had slowly dissolved
  & it was no safer outside the museum where Ilse

the fräulein who took care of me when mother worked
took me to her Black Forest house with the ceramic
German stove for cooking children in the middle of her
        bedroom—When I was asleep she put two hot bricks
        at my feet & roasted me as her porcelain dolls shrieked
In those days under every bed
was an enormous chamber pot held down by angels
in which lived a fin-de-siècle monster filled with children's
        brains—And all these were glazed & shiny & full of history.
In a country where there weren't many things
where the material world was both thin & threadbare—
you could easily see the light shining through it—
we loved & feared our chamber pots and stoves fiercely
even as we could not remember what was written on them.
But things were certainly written on them
and those few of us who knew how to read read them
without surcease. Ilse, for instance, read Gothic script
to me in the Bruckenthal, intoning Mittle Deutsch like a Latin mass—
And now & then in the chiaroscuro of the Bruckenthal which was
        saving money on lights I would encounter an old scholar
        named Ferenc Pasperger who always made notes & wore a coat
        so shiny & so thin you could see his yellow parchment skin
        underneath. One afternoon he bid me put my ear to the bulge
        of a pot that was quite a bit taller than me
        & had grooves on its fat belly. "Listen!" he said. I listened.
I heard something like a far-off sea something I'd heard before
        in seashells. I told him so. "No, listen deeper!" he said,
        and as I did it seemed to me that I heard voices talking,
        shouting, laughing at some great distance, behind a wall.
I heard children. "That's it! That's it!" said Ferenc, his bony
        forehead close to mine. "Those are," he said, "the voices
        of the people who made this pot, and you can hear their
        children talking, and whoever was around just then."
It was true. I listened most of that afternoon and heard people

long dead conversing in the pot.
Ferenc thought that the grooves were like grooves on a record
    and that the makers of the pots used their tools to record
    their worlds, and that we could hear them if we listened.
And that fired my imagination & I thought that I could listen
    to Socrates, for instance, if only I found the right pot
    because he hung out in the market around the pot makers
    & the mob, or to anyone for that matter, and that I could
    pick up the secrets whispered within range of the turning stylus:
    hints of hidden treasure, plots to kill, the mumbled seeds
    of conversation that became *Gilgamesh,* or *Don Quixote* or
    The Last Testament of François Villon—
And ever since then I've been listening. I put my ear to the old
    pots and hear the vanished people gab. And sometimes I pick
    them up, the great and the not so great dead I steal
    my verses from—
Hidden on dishes, pots and sculptures in plain sight
is our history and our peculiar rhythms—

I also found a little later—
I was growing up fast in those days—
that in the old cemetery
among the amputated angels and the listing urns
were ideal places to hide with a girl.
I hid there with Aurelia.
One summer afternoon she and I lay on the bodies
of two knights carved with their arms crossed
on their tombstones
who made a low sorrowful moan of long gone love
until we tumbled between them and there on the broke
debris we commenced the old dance.
Many times the startled angels sighed and fell
off their pedestals while the urns tipped as our hot
fire passed through them.

And then it rained & you could hear the dead
straining to leave the squishy slimy squeaky mud
and to burst their bonds of crumbling stone
as we continued
working the clay and the shards with our bodies
until it was time to go home and catch hell—
those days were full of cracked & babbling ceramics,
urns, jugs & broken pillars to hide behind—
we were like statues or dolls ourselves:
still when the adults were watching
& animated & full of an insane music when they were not.

Having decided to be a poet for reasons having to do
partly with all the whispering text about me
and partly because I was full like a jug with
all the milk of my adolescence
I began putting words on paper
though only incidentally on paper—
I would have liked to write on clay tablets.
Failing that I would
have liked to inscribe the bowls
we slurped our gruel from so that in getting to the bottom
the startled glutton would be confronted suddenly
with his won mortality: "He who made this bowl
salutes you. From now on you are his. Obey his oracle,
you greedy dog!" Or: "You've gotten to the bottom. From
here on out only the journey matters."
In the fifties communism achieved a Zen-like simplicity.
It was every man and his bowl.
And it was every woman and her single potato
or, on holidays, a bone.
Books were even scarcer.
The only things to read were signs from the past.

And these were written on dishes kept under lock and key.
And on small things that fell on us in the cemetery
from the toppled funeraria: old coins, spiders, withered hearts,
dried livers and coarse spiny flowers.

Consequently, our imaginations were free to spin.
We spun imaginary beings which
unlike the flesh ones are always spun not born.
We were all mind potters turning the wheels of our
blooming flesh into a void made cold by ideology.
And it was a muddy world too because as soon
as you left the dimly lit city with her cracked pavements
and her crackling, sighing and swaying cemetery
you were back in the stew-thick dark of peasant villages
yoked to skinny nags and sluggish oxen
whose job was not to pull these villages anywhere
into, let's say the 20th century
but the keep them anchored rather
to the Carpathian mountains—
they groaned there at the heart
of dismembered feudal estates,
shadowed by monasteries and castles perched on crags—
in one of these at Argeş
a young girl had been built alive into the wall
so that the wall would stand—
and in another Countess Bathory drank
the blood of 650 virgin girls
in order to keep her youth—
and ghosts were still drinking from stone cups
a substance that could have been time itself—
they did not care about communism
they looked rather into a farther past
for that single object, the Grail, and its connection

to god, or some god, or some essential magic.

It can be argued of course that the Grail was itself
capitalism, that its function was to transform the creative
blood or sweat of the divine into the multitude
of objects that fill the world now. the alchemists'
alembics, grinders, mortars, pestles and jars, moved
steadily toward the generative heard of matter where
the pure transformative operation percolated in its sealed
container. Not far from us, in Prague, a rabbi
made a man of clay called a Golem and gave him life
by writing the name of God on his forehead, and when
this lyric statuette began behaving badly the rabbi
did to him what god did to us. He erased the word
and the creature crumbled.

Communism was a golem by the midsixties.
It awaited only the hand to erase the word.
God had pretty much been done away with by then
both in the East and the West.
After a time the unsettled creation
that had issued from the lord's kilns
came to the rather
chilling conclusion
that only the murder of God could
restore it to paradise. This conclusion, I must add, was
chilling but inevitable, given the magnitude of our loss
and the grudge we carried ever since we were hurled
like cheap Napoleons from our golden-pot selves into
the muck of history,
the story of which we have scratched into every
available surface
and would have continued to do so to this day
had history not ended & the electronic media

taken its place.
But that's another story.
In the intervening centuries
between the Fall & the deicide
we elaborated our revenge—
by the middle of the 19th we had it—
we did to God what he did to us—
we pulled God out of the heavens
and when he fell he too broke into a thousand shards—
that's why there are so many god-struck people now.
This was but simple justice though it is nice that we observed
        the forms
and had Nietzche sign the official death certificate.
These god-struck people with god-shards
        imbedded in their brains
amble about in large numbers
        while the larger shards
float above their heads and are called flying saucers
        and in this form are seen daily by millions
in the sky and the popular press—
        Though it could also be the case
that some of these saucers were made by ceramicists
        in California & loosed upon the rest of us.
                                (You know who you are!)

The 19th century happened for me around my 19th year.

It is not coincidental that both the 19th century
        and my 19th year
were the sites of an overwhelming profusion of dishes,
pots and soup tureens, broken gravestone angels,
leaf-stuffed gargoyles trying to cough them out,
clay-born worlds
that multiplied in panic and in response

to chimney stacks and factories—
the Victorian world was making a last stand for the handmade
craft in the kitchens and the boudoirs
which gave birth to Freud—
while out of the smoking chimneys of mass production
Karl Marx was born—
and as for me I was considering marrying Aurelia the girl
from my hometown whose dowry
consisted of one hundred plates
displaying Minoan-like fertility charms
ancient designs that came from Minos via Illyria to Dacia Felix
two marble jars that looked Cretan,
a serpentine goblet that could have been used in Babylonia,
and two hundred black bowls with a red glaze
matched by two hundred cups
with a snake beneath each handle—
an incredible wealth that had come unbroken
through her mountain-folk who had traded
sheep for centuries in the Black Sea–Mediterranean world
where eventually the amphoras of Greece, Rome and Byzantine
encountered the spice jars, oil jugs and wine goblets of the
  Orient, including those huge Arabian Nights pots where Ali
  Baba and the forty thieves hid—

even as the rest of her mother's culture lay in shards
all about her—
her mother worked in a textile factory.
In the end it was all for the best.
We would not have gotten along
and all those dishes would have doubtless
broken on the shoals of our stormy relationship.

I took my writing tablets elsewhere then—
to the West
to a world of happy plastic

a universe of Melmac,
nylon, vinyl lounge chairs,
naugah interiors and lava lamps
where the products of ersatz Freud
reclined, sipping chemicals
through plastic straws,
from tall mass-produced goblets.
This was the Dow Country
the country of Dow Chemicals and napalm.

Thank God for the hippies.
And for Latin America.
In potters' sheds a secret nation
the children of the plastic people
were making another world
out of clay.
In California I lived with several potters
who made self-refilling coffee mugs, bottomless
        bean pots, self-cleaning ashtrays & vanishing tea cups
that imparted to the tea-drinkers an uncanny Japanese style
        kind of peace that after surpassing all understanding
        led to some fabulous Kabuki-like theatre & sex.
And when my friends talked about their pots it always sounded
to me as if they were talking about sex:
they said wide shoulders, thickened mouth rim, cobalt
        blue under the glaze, long neck, undulating rim, deeply
        recessed, high flaring foot, and once there was
        buff stoneware covered with a white slip. That one
        really got me.
And I could see how one could fall in love with a pot as if it
        were a person & many of my friends who
were in fact in love with pots were a lot less damaged
        than the human fauna that spinned about the place.
And my wife Alice had a dream about a village clustered around

a pyramid atop which wise elders sat smoking and chatting
and she spent the next year making it: a multitude of villagers
engaged in tasks about the wells and the fields, women cooking
children dancing in a circle, people staring out the windows
& in the middle was the pyramid and the elders &
she called this The Clay People's Republic &
when she finished it I had a dream that all the people
who ever lived were now here again made out of clay
awaiting only a signal to start going about their business
& I woke up wondering how we would all fit
on the same earth which is getting smaller as I speak—
In Mexico just across the way
a myriad of gods, goddesses, and fetishes
also came out of the ground
and out of kilns
in a jumble of archeology & modernity
pre-Colombian past below
insurgent new muralista colors above.
I saw a terra-cotta dog with a human mask
made in Colima
a native hairless dog
and a clay model of an Aztec ball court
with eager spectators
and countless males and females holding
things that looked like rockets—
and clay masks
and priests, shamans, nobles, and peasants,
whole worlds, friendly and unfriendly,
representing the seen and the unseen—

but most of all I saw myself
seated at a stall in a plaza of the New World
writing letters for hire for illiterate lovers
while underneath my papers was a stone tablet

on which the writing I did on paper
inscribed itself simultaneously in a cuneiform-type language
that only few could read.
And I became quite the fetishist as you can see.
And in 1989 communism collapsed,
the word gone from its forehead.
The borders of the empires blurred.
The clays across official borders
became visible, an intermingling
that could be fertile & rich.
But simultaneously the pots of small nations
rose from their buried hovels full
of the unsettled honey of a thousand lost wars.
These drums of tightly packed sentiment & hate
are now being carried on the shoulders of hungry mobs
who want the opened, worshipped, and divined.
How we break them open without destroying their beauty
or mocking their pain
is the challenge of our art—

My friends, potters digging up the earth,
leaving holes in it until the whole mass of it
becomes artifact or art
you must divine the vectors of its new order—
that's the price for not keeping still in paradise.

After words ceramics are the most legible writing
and words themselves are written mostly upon the dishes
to which I keep my ear,
and what they say is,
it's a long story of mud & of hands
and the hands that fashion the mud refashion the world—
when little hands play in the clay
they make monsters and warriors who pummel each other
who have names & things to say to each other

273

and twirling ballerinas and princesses who also
have names & things to say to each other
& in play all return to childhood
even self-intoxicated adolescents in their cups
who think a lot about god

that poor god without a pot to piss in
whose shards are now everywhere to be found

COMRADE PAST & MISTER PRESENT

INTRODUCTION

• *Comrade Past & Mister Present*
  Minneapolis: Coffee House Press, 1986 (Editor: Allan Kornblum)

Allan Kornblum and I had been friends for a decade before he pub-
lished this book. We first met at his house in West Branch, Iowa,
where he wrote, edited, and printed on letterpress his own work,
and that of his friends, the Actualists. The philosophical chief of the
Actualist movement was the much missed Darrel Grey, who defined
Actualism as doing "to things what light does to them," a paraphrase
of a verse by Guillevic. As we were heading into the nineties, the
world was, once more, changing. There was new optimism in the air,
as well as a new sobriety, and the beginning of a revolution in the
seemingly monolithic Soviet Bloc. Romania, my birthplace, seemed
the most stolidly frozen of the commie empire's regions, but even
there a new spirit was quietly brewing. My own life took several turns
toward respectability: I started teaching literature and writing, first at
Johns Hopkins University in Baltimore, where John Barth hired me
for two years as "writer in residence"; then at the University of
Baltimore; and finally, at Louisiana State University in Baton Rouge,
where I taught for twenty-five years until I retired in 2009. In 1983 I
founded *Exquisite Corpse: A Journal of Books & Ideas*, a literary journal
ambitiously intended as a monthly, but which ended up, manageably,
a quarterly, and a "Journal of Letters and Life" when I moved to
Louisiana. In 1983 I also began writing weekly newspaper columns on
art and life, first in the *City Paper*, then the *Baltimore Evening Sun*, and
finally in the *Baltimore Sun*. One of these columns ended up being
read on the air on National Public Radio's *All Things Considered*,
where I delivered a weekly commentary for over thirty years. The

marvelous thing about this journalism was that I wasn't in any way constrained or censored by my editors, and I was left to rant and rave at my pleasure, often coming close to the obscure syntax of pure poetry. If poetry was 100 percent whiskey, some of my journalism was at least 70 percent alcohol, and that was only because I felt obliged to use complete sentences. Keeping up with the world of news turned out to be immensely beneficial in the coming decade, when I was able to "cover" and witness firsthand the collapse of state communism in Romania and travel widely with radio and televison producers. My notebooks were a jumble of poetry lines, quotes from an amazing variety of people, and impressions of places that tourists never saw. My "Comrade Past" self was quickly morphing into a hard-working "Mister Present."

dear masoch

Dear Masoch doodling with his contracts
pens Venus in Furs on the margin of the document
he is preparing where it says
how many lashes he must receive, and where,
when the door opens & in the gaping doorway
a head framed by Viennese blue says:

"I am a Girl in Search of an Interpretation
filled with creamy snow like a vanilla éclair
I am waiting in the window of the dusty
European Poetry Shop for a soldier
to bring the following question before us:

'What do you do if you're a masochist but have been placed
in a position of power?' "

The girl who is the skinny international type
as yet unknown for another century
but whose prototype is already visible
in certain forward-looking writers like Madame de Staël
who is taking the species from courtesanship
to traveler's checks
hides behind dark glasses and travels with only a toothbrush
and a diaphragm in her straw bag,
objects unknown as well although their prototypes
in the form of rough twigs smeared with dental powder
and sea sponges soaked in torn anemones
have been in Masoch's house before.

She has power over boys and is equally at home with money.
He says:

"You must use your power to draw contracts specifying the amount
of prose I mean pain you want inflicted on yourself."

She is leaning on a cardboard structure waiting
for him to take her photograph and to sever the strings
by which the large balloon tied to the structure
is lightly attached and when sufficiently airborne
to take hold of her feet and kiss them.
The life of her soles flickers briefly above him
like the life of dreams flickers above all tales
& glows after they are told, for a second.
Her entire world is covered with graffiti. They say
Read Me. Interpret Me. He will. He does. He lifts the glass
paperweight holding down the poem and out the window
it flutters. Her damp pulse is in evolutionary
overdrive.
"They imagine they think," she says.
"I can get around reason as easily as Nietzsche
gets around his house to meet his fate. Or face,
as my mother says. 'You must have face!' 'With
face all things are possible!' If action is
the unreasoned interpretation of my position
whose oddity is beginning to bother me, then we are all
in the interpretation business. The reasoned
readings should, according to the interests
of the reader, be either weighed down or inevitable,
so either let go of my foot or cut the strings."

It is a moment filled for Masoch with the rapture
of understanding nothing. Therefore he leans on the
poetic misappropriation of his youth by certain

aborted flights of reactionary romanticism
and pours out of himself:

"Oh, but I want to be thin and filled
with your doomed elegance like *filet de* swan, like
old verse in the corrupted daycore . . . fancy
the daycore when I am through with you!"

The barely heard music of the threat is not lost
on the aspiring masochist. She too
is leaning on an obsolete tradition
instead of going to law school:

"A man furnishes his heart with explanations.
There, the chair. That's where the mirror goes."

"In a cheap hotel."

"So cheap I dread to think of the knives glinting
from the unbuckled belts of torn pants—men lurking
in the dim one-watt light bulb halls soggy
with blood their carpets still fresh from recent
beatings and forced strippings
the doors impossible to latch the windows painted shut
with an intoxicating lead-based paint
the bed sheets—what is left of them!—displaying
maps of terræ incognitæ in sperm and constellations
in blood drawn by either lice or the monthlies of
street women or forcibly taken virgins
and the constant hum! the screaming of busted
water pipes the moans of the dying junkie next door
the impossible visions of the nymphomaniac drinking in
three burly men at once, a fight on the street.
And then I see the terror on your face as you lie

under me being ridden like a nasty nag to your doom:
'What is the matter, scum?' I ask and follow
your terror-crazed eyes to the ceiling where they rest
on a monstrous *fleur-du-mal* painted on the ceiling
with human blood and brains. It appears
that someone lying on this very bed
put a gun under their chin or in their mouth
and decorated the ceiling thus. 'Oh!' and I can
feel it, the elusive gift of total surrender
as two prongs like a snail's horns shoot out of my
clitoris and antennae-like begin to pick up the beat
from the far-off galaxy where I really live."

"And then just as my terror is transformed as well
into the pleasure of having fulfilled my contract . . . "

Masoch waves the contract in the air.

"You get up, pull up your little flowered undies
and leave, slamming the door behind you so that
a few chips of ceiling blood flake over me like snow
and I must stay there, like that, egglike
for at least fifty years until psychoanalysis
becomes a respectable profession and a psycho-
analyst a person one can call from a hotel
in the middle of the night, even in Marseilles."

"In all this," she says separately, to someone apart,
"Reason looms separate and voluntary like a fruit
in a rabbinical garden, or braces on the teeth
of Mormon belles. We are none too sure if the
Mongolians we imitate know how to read, and I don't
like yogurt. And I assume that reading,"
she turns the page

"is all there is, even if I'm awake. Especially
then. Can fresh water make it seem like next day?
I know who's listening and I came too soon.
The holes in space are purring like a cat, calling
attention to their idealism or their exactness
They don't breathe too hard, or too slow, they are
not in a hurry, there is a universe next door,
a reversible fragment. Refreshed, after she slept,
Reason awoke to find Goya's monsters perfectly
appropriate, artistically drawn, and all that,
and in her mental baggage. Get those things out
of here! she cries. I will not rest until I make
an aphorism as good as those they have assigned
to me, and on she goes, I mean on I go, insisting
on the right to a nearly empty straw bag over
my shoulder, and a passport. I tell you, the original
mistake of philosophers is to keep silent
on music and on cars."

Misguided Masoch holds the trembling rifle he's been
holding for an hour, hoping to shoot Karl Marx. From
the dusty hideout in the fork of a twisted olive above
a farmer's pigsty, he calls to the thin shadow slowly
going from him like an effete oxcart:
"Untranslatable you! Banal futurism! Our paper servers
are combing the future for you! You are hardly
capable of understanding anything except your little
beastie-in-residence! You have been infected by the
legalization of pain and are no more than a bored fire
burning itself out in the bush alone, without a city,
firemen, great engines, excitement, and the press. The
overstimulated mind elite of which I was once part
is no more. We have taken to the twisted branches
of the olives with rifles. There is action in us! Oh

yeah! There is a kind of sleep in us from which
you will be born. I love you."

There is a brief report. A dove with a bullet in her
beak flies away. The two wws in the form of two fat crows
stand on the branch above Masoch and chatter in frigid
vulgate. A caterpillar that is actually a grenade pin
pulls himself slowly out, and the explosion is loud
enough to eliminate the peasantry and rearrange the
geodemographics of the world. Of course, none of this
bothers Masoch. His name is immortal, and the contracts
he has drawn standard. The striped fields cross
the sentence in the hand-held word-mixer searching
like floodlights for the skinny psychopath from another
century who stands in her kitchen under a meteorite
shower mixing herself a Margarita. The urgency holds
her breath as she passes from the gates of metaphor
to the little Formica table where the sun shines
so lovely in the a.m. There is a chipped vase with
field flowers in it, some wilting, and a handful
of scallions rising next to it like the African
proletariat who never panned out. Deadjectified
she leans limply on the sill of her youth. She could
zip up her parka & mount the demented tractor still
and consider the transmission and love, which is
a motor function, but it is too late. The revolution
has subdivided her into dumber & dumber characters
like a trompe l'oeil landscape composed of zillions
of theories, which she could think of as either
grist for the mill, or angels. In either case she
is a boss and an employer. Her passport has been
canceled, she can drink her drink overtly for the use
of money, or covertly for the repopulation
of the planet with tiny insectlike machine people

forcibly pulled out of the planetary psyche
which, empty, reels like a great revolver chamber
filled with the souls' ungraspable trajectories,
or she could in extremis call for her flesh
and for the bitter conclusion of her contract
with Masoch, which is death.

"None of that," she calls from the doorway
under the blossoming arbor where she has set
up an alternative to the hotel rooms of Marseilles.
"No dread sobriety should attend the gestures
of those present, no one should signal intently
to something out of sight, there will be no taxi
obscured by a tree with the motor running. No
furrowed brows ploughed under by thought, no
pajamas. No obvious seeds sprouting discreet
flowers, no discreet flowers at all. Only grotesque
flowers like one-eyed Susans, the floral cyclopes. No
gents with violets, only gentians with mimosas. Only
uncertain professions, no new branches of mental
hygiene. No sulphur baths, no inception of chills, no
thermometers. No chilly languages, no translations
from chilly texts. No translators catching colds
from opening windows between languages, no crossroads,
only real stammerings, true hollows where the tongues
stand in their cases heavy with the awkward honey
of the first spoken, the as-yet-unsaid, the moist
dimensions, childhoods with animals, childhoods
that are great battles not preventive thoughts,
there on streets that can't exist, igniting
themselves with food mass-produced from all the nos
& no-nos a woman & her dummy can attract in a long
& unruly life, a river of charm, really."

Her voice runs from her like a monk pursued
by a buggering papyrus. Why are we not
in this book? cry her lovers. Because, she says,
without this time opening her chapped quotation
marks, those I love quietly do not textify
as readily as those who cause disturbances,
men like Masoch here, and other literary figures
whose photos I collect. All these guys do is
talk poems with big P as if the A-bomb wasn't
capital enough. Guided by styles, imagined
buildings, things impossible to draw, idiot
fantasies, wallowing in the rejecta of their
childhoods, they have originally happened
to someone else. To me they are semaphorisms,
crustaceans renegotiating the order of isms,
who have died for something in the future, some-
thing Sundaylike but juicy, the skin of something
basic and direct, why beat around the bush: me.
What good is the good horseman after he lost
his head? Plenty, say I, both the crazed horse
and the head that goes on thinking, rolling
crazed eyes at the border guard who wants to see
inside. They all want to see inside, it becomes
necessary to see inside every minute, then every
second it becomes necessary to see what's new,
or if the old is quaint yet, or if the dream
of lit has added anything since the oral rap
of certain marsupials. The fear is always
that we might go away before we figured out
why we came in the first place. That we might
run out of text in the flower of our youth,
not like Keats running out of youth in the flower
of his text. That we would crouch behind an unrehearsed
bit of prose, ready to pounce on the slightest

poem biking by, only to find that sentences
stretch into years, that years flow into pages,
that the world gets erased as quickly as we type,
that no one types, that a large gaze holds us
transfixed in its unblinking, flat look. You
really want me to put you in this book?

Having taken full advantage of her escape
from quotes, she stretches under the waterfall
of Masoch's steady penmanship under a backdrop
of Toledo swords and hears the pirouetting
of her shadow in his sleep, a sound like that
of a young Arab crouching behind a garage.

What legal needs I have, spoke Masoch from his branch,
which, used with the one below, served him
for the quotation marks he too had just escaped,
have been vastly rankled by the future
which responds only to forced entry and is
always the enterer, not the entree. Therefore
I'll charge myself a fee for every error of fact
and give myself a whipping for every odd fancy.
The State is a terminal cancer, it sucks
the lollipops of our souls, it sits on our skulls.
She does not exist.

Oh, but I do.

the fourth of july
for Ted Berrigan, July 4, 1983

I know a sad and large man who lives in West Germany.

That's how I thought I would start a newspaper article about a man I don't know, a Romanian poet who sends me his sad self-published little books every three months or so. This man is a doctor, a G.P. probably in a small coal-mining German town. I see the post office where he buys his stamps and gets his mail and the little coffee shop where he has his schwarzen Kaffee and writes his sad poems. His poems aren't just sad, they are desolate, they are haunted, they are hollow and ground down, the despair is thick and incontrovertible. There are leaden seas and hopeless rivers in them and burnt trees with dots of pain on the charred branches. The humans are missing from his landscapes as resolutely as if they'd been rubbed out so long ago nobody even remembers them. But once in a while a remarkable little human thought will make its appearance, astonishing in its petty incomprehension. Things like: "They've thought of it, so now I have to eat it." Does he have a wife, children? Probably.

Today is the Fourth of July. The radio plays the "Ode to Anacreon," from which F. S. Key took "The Star-Spangled Banner." I'm an American, no doubt about it. My heart swells with pride at this brass riot, I am transported. I love Mr. Jefferson. A genius. A revolutionary. A great visionary. He would have puked on Ronald Reagan. He would have put little Ronnie on one of his enormous, historical knees and puked the remains of an immense vegetarian meal washed down with grog on Ronnie's little head. Ronnie should be so lucky!

Whenever I go into a school, I try to get maximum erotic charge from youth, so I compose odes that correct the obvious inconvenience of actual bodies and their deformities. Only rarely among youth, in schools, do you actually *see* a shining body or mind. You just suspect that they are there, because they *have* to be. So sayeth all of folklore. So sayeth your old mind. So you bring out these things that all these things sayeth by means of odes.

> Always use their typewriters
> They will never be the same
> Stoned keys the silent arbiters
> Of dangers hidden in a name.

> Not that the poem comes out best
> In jail, but under the piano or
> In the dusty street where the rest
> Roll back eggs into the nest

> Of a fact in the sidebar of a news-
> Letter being put together by young
> Bodies complicated not obtuse
> Transparent, sincere, oh skinny tang!

How silly. But you can bring out youth by these semihermetic means, if only because curiosity makes a creature bloom. But I'm not even being amused. I simply suffer the ignominy of cuteness, the futility of pretending something for a bit, a tiny bit of money. Meanwhile, the children, the bodies I am teaching are immensely rich. Half the children are millionaires themselves, the other half's parents are. There are Mercedeses, Cadillacs, Jaguars parked in the school lot. You can hear a kind of contented gurgle, the flowing of milk through the well-worn channels of oligarchic tranquillity. There are names here that go back to the founding days of the Republic, traditions tighter than a harness on a cavalry horse. The military, business, and managerial castes have money riding on these children. Indeed, they ride *on* money, like wagons on rails. The youth I am trying to bring out is the youth that is being ground out of them by means of a rigorous education. The forms of youth are set, the manifestations coded, the clothes prescribed, the limits defined. I'm a fool, in the English office, with an old typewriter.

I can imagine this little West German doctor, this terrible poet, this sad caricature in Germany, the Germany of the post-post-miracle. The burghers are only now awakening from the postwar miracle, and they find themselves to be little Americans! Cubed houses, disposable cars, fast food! But they are only formally Americans, Americans without Mr. Jefferson. Inside, they are nobody. At the center of the nobodyness of their hollow insides sits this sweating little immigrant, this sloppy fat doctor writing his desolate, horrid, hopelessness-filled works. He is like a wafting of bombed basement, this little foreigner, his dark eyes darting between one hollow breast to another of the mastectomized owner of the little café where he likes his schwarzen Kaffee hot. He knows that her breasts are only rubber balloons: he ordered them for her by mail, and he adjusts them every month.

The radio hostess was so-o-o thrilled to have me on her show. It was like having a doll or a new dress, something so-o-o exciting! I had it in my mind to make her laugh. It was, ultimately, too easy. She was already laughing when I went in. She laughed all the way through the introduction, then laughed at her own question, then literally *cracked up*—her makeup opened up like an earthquake into myriad gray lines—and she *kept* cracking up. It was epic, completely out of proportion with what I heard myself saying, which was nothing. "Read to me," she said, "something from your pockets." I'd just told her that my pockets were filled with art, notes, poems, that they were veritable mines full of treasures, all one had to do was dig, dig. I put my hands into the left mine, pushed past South Africans with headlights, and pulled this out and read:

"All have secrets who have experienced inexpressible things. A secret is what has no language. Morons have the most secrets. The NSA and the CIA, which have the most secrets, are the world's biggest morons. After that come poets, who are forever struggling with the inexpressible and are only capable of small portions of it, meagre meals to be sure."

"Oh! Oh! That's so-o-o! Read it again, please!"

I read:

"Everything is inexpressible. Morons are walking bombs bursting with secrets. We sat down at a meal of filet moron and were quickly imbued with mystery, soaked in essence, perforated by the elsewhere."

Behind the twinkling eyes of the radio hostess, the automatic question-making machine broke down, and for a moment the wires showed. Through the cracks in her makeup I saw someone squatting on the ground in August, making peepee, while enormous black clouds covered the earth. Soon it was going to rain.

Kansas is as big as the world.

Either I have been blessed with content or cursed with it. Whichever way you look at it, it's work. Without content it's easier work, dependent on other means of support, some of them truly undignified. With content it's a mixture of work and some of the easiness of non-content. The payoff of content is fame, money, immortality, a seat at the circus.

Like flowers growing out of thin air, or enormous vegetables in outer space with their roots showing like the obscene nerves of molars, the little West German exile's poems grow and scintillate with a life of their own, nourished by a deep fake memory, no talent and no music, in and of themselves like Leibniz's spheres. He admires their growth, despises himself, bows to the other customers. It's closing time at the sad café in the sad little provincial town in little America Germany. Everyone now must go home to their cement cubes to turn on the TV. The proprietess thrusts her rubber balloons provocatively forward as she wipes the spot of dry schwarzen Kaffee on the marble top. With a sudden gesture the poet sticks his fork into one of them. It deflates with a sad hiss, letting out sad years of marital juggling, pastel dreams, a variety of mouths stuck at various angles of greed, their teeth shining and showing, and air. *"Oh, mein Gott!"* mumbles the terrified poet. "Frau Goebbels! I didn't mean to!" He takes his poor head between his sweaty, trembling palms and, with a resolute gesture, pulls it off his neck and, in the same movement, lifts the blouse of the proprietess and sticks it in there where the deflated breast can be heard breathing its last pfffssst! It is, needless to say, a huge head, completely out of proportion with the other rubber breast, giving her, momentarily, a grotesque appearance. It has all happened so fast! Frau Goebbels is so astonished, she has not stopped wiping the spot of schwarzen Kaffee on the marble top. But it's a fact: the head of the poet is now the left breast of the café owner. And there is terrible disproportion between left and right, a kind of monstrous political imbalance possible only in Germany.

I meet a friend of mine downtown for coffee. This friend of mine is a poet who has been in school for a very long time. He has a degree in poetry. He writes a very precise kind of poetry that is very much like the poetry other school poets write. His poetry is very comical, actually, but he thinks of it as at least profound, if not tragic. He is all worked up over a parable he has found in a story by Borges, a parable that concerns him personally.

It appears that a king had commissioned a poetic battle from a poet. The poet came back with a great poem full of great poetic victories. The king gave him a mirror, told him to go away. Ten years later, the poet returns with the battle. He reads it to the king, and it *is* the battle. The king gives him a gold mask. The poet goes away for another ten years, whispers something in the king's ear, and kills himself. The king gives up kinging, becomes a beggar, and wanders about in rags.

"And," my friend said, "I'm now working to become perfect at the battle, so I could get the mask!"

I felt suddenly very sorry for him. All that schooling wasted. All that dedication coming to naught.

"Listen," I said, "that mask is only a medal of service. The poet had only managed to return the mirror to the king so the king could see himself. So he gave him a medal of service to the state because he'd finally learned how to politick and flatter. Alas, the poet was only a poet when he brought in the first poem. After that, he was only a courtier and a vassal."

"How about the last part?" the poet protested vehemently. "Isn't the king wise to give up? And isn't the poet wise?"

"That last part is disgusting," I said. "Of course, old men become wise. What else can they become with a foot, a hand, and a tongue in the grave? Still, the poet is wiser than the king because he has the good sense to go in search of the unknown. The king just walks around hoping to hear from the dead, which is probably what the poet promised him, that he would come back in another ten years with the news, if not a new poem. And the fool king believes him."

"That's terrible," the poet says. "Do you want to talk about something else?"

Never. I never want to talk. I throw the waitress an evil look and leave.

The proprietess, left hanging there with uneven breasts, faced the West German without a head, trying in vain to look into his eyes. She would have done better to lift her blouse and look into his eyes there. But then a miracle happened. The head began to shrink. No, the other breast began to grow.

No, the head began to shrink. No. And so on. I could care less.

A sudden rain is going to drown out the fireworks at the harbor. But the radio goes on, playing my song.

music

There were no bums in my pores.
New York had opened my pores & bedenimed & bendovered
    walked in my fantasies
        shoving bums.
The stores were open and the hours late.
Expectations were being fed
        not sent to work
        like in far-away San Francisco.
I could speed up & slow down
    grimace & guffaw
        move my hands
           & look up to the lit windows
filled with admiration for the natives
    though not wanting to be asked in
since my living room at the moment was the biggest.
I was digging the streets & the streets dug me.
Every lunatic sped toward its co-lunatic.
Bellevue was lit up like another apartment building
    & in fact a party of sorts was going on
        with the inmates happy to be warm
           even as they were being hurt.
Ambulances piled in front & people went in & a few
           came out
    & the enormous hallways could have fit
      a Communist city
      which they did
because on several floors the inmates slept there.
But these hallways were dirty green & bright yellow

& the neon was dirty
    & the unhappy floors
were track-marked by wheelchairs & police boots
    & mad jigs
      & flares & broken glass.
The floor to be sure was a picture of hell.
The prison ward was behind two tall gates &
    wire-mesh windows
      an easy jail break
& the cops were half cops & half social workers
    & in go the two poet workers
      with their two culture cops, i.e., books
& there are the prisoners
    half wanting to look at a woman
      & half desirous to look at free folk
& half sick of each other
    & half sick
& half serious criminals
    wanting to improve their lot in life
& half mad criminals
    who had it in for the other half.
One came with a bed and a trapeze for his bandaged arm
    & half a body in a cast
& another walked in wheeling a tall steel cane
on a flying saucer from which flew an IV bag connected
    to his arm
& as he walked
    he recited bathroom walls
but was interrupted in mid-rhyme
    by an atmosphere of human color
    occasioned mostly by a reader of best-sellers
    who wanted to write them
because he had lived dramatically & was interested
    in technique & his interest

led to metaphysical questions
        which gave the poets a license to interrupt.
Another was grim & tall & black
        & in his head he carried
the entire philosophy of an obscure mystical sect
        in severe couplets:
"In the middle of the pyramid there is an eye.
The dollar bill has a lookout in the fourth sky.
The steps to the Capitol are seventy-three.
That is the number to cross the zebra & the flea."
    I am probably being unjust
        to a grim mystical doctrine
            which the man whispered
                before being led out
                    by Big Sister
                        in mid-rhyme.
It was an evening to forget & one to remember.
It was 9:45 & the night was young.
At 10:25 I had collected myself sufficiently to return
    to the world hopeful
        & why not
when so many were rhyming the world in their heads
    even on their back & in bandages
& while you can't call this feeling love
    there being no room for close-up oppression
there was a hope that half was not lost.
Parts of the Sunday newspapers still covered the city.
The stores were open & a thousand ways to get high too.
Denizens of the night revealed fragments of wild costumes.
In the bookstores an intellectual orgy raged.
The smell of pastry & coffee was being attacked by ginger
        & Mongolian pepper
            from inside red restaurants.
It was possible to consume everything or nothing.

Either way the balance was righted
    the consumers as passionate as the ascetics.
The Lower East Side of New York
    moved eternally by a rhythm
  "beating outside ordinary time"
        no shit
            the graces of cheapness.
Cheap were the pirogis
    at the Kiev.
Cheap pirogis at the Kiev
    6 boiled with sour cream $1.95
a whole subclass converted to Ukrainian food
    & this without pamphlets
        or monks,
each pirogi a pamphlet-monk
    doing its preaching in the mouth:
"if the Ukraine is ever to be free
        you must eat all your pirogi"
though there are people who do not like them
because they have first seen them fried
which is not always the best way to make somebody's acquaintance
not a pamphlet-monk's certainly
        & halfway through my second pirogi
            the radio said John Lennon was shot.
John Lennon was shot by an assassin.
Minutes later the radio said he was critically wounded.
And later yet that he was dead.
        The waiter held his plates in abeyance
            & his face became very sad
                & a tear fell on a pirogi
            & I was still hopeful but shocked.
A man named Chapman meaning chap man man man anyman
            "I am no man"
        a failed double with a gun

a fallen half
had been shooting at a symbol & killed Lennon instead.
And now his music came from the sidewalks
      & everyone understood
        & became much sadder
          & their tears fell
on solid gold pirogis rolling into image-making machines.
The symbolists had killed John Lennon
    & I thought
    look at it as a vacancy
    a power vacuum
    a king is dead
    it will make everyone think
    for a few seconds before commerce sets in
      & that's no way to think
        but it was thinking me.
Chapman was now in Bellevue where I had been
      11:15 p.m. Monday, December 8
  an hour earlier
    with the other halved halves
& the hairs on my arm stood over the pirogis
    when I remembered that it was here
      in the Kiev
        ten years ago
          that I'd heard of Bobby Kennedy's death
which at the time struck me like the free winds of doom
    with the apocalyptic illumination
      of anarchist Jews.
Ah cheap pirogis in love with yourselves!
I was in love but with no one in particular.

petite madeleine

We never discuss tenancy
We are a most peculiar couple
Our street isn't on the map

I remember kissing you
Form is punishment
The being compelled to it

Pays in full for the sizzling
Neuron grid clamped tight
On the cracked map

If you do what you think
You have to you can modernize
Yourself all on your own

Cooked in the end by micro-
Waves sweet fleeing monk
Buggered by papyrus

With first act of play on it
Performed by ancient photog-
Raphers in the loud mud

Of Egypt Mesopotamia Babylon
Dacia Illyria Thrace Baton Rouge
Mass-produced blow job's

First Henry Ford a cosmopolitan
Criminal in Communist journalism
Walking to and fro in the glass

Aquarium of agents in the know
This street can't exist
So let's do it again

Doubling the windows and the bricks
Turning the vibrant hermeneut
Loose on the twelve-story building

Each story a bit peculiar
Self-told but totally dependent
On its mad teller's psycho-

Analysis like an I-told-you-so
Told in a thousand languages
A million inflections

Still what was it I told you
In the first place second third
I kissed you you had your orders

comrade past & mister present

Can the misfortune of a dog owned by vegetarians
be felt by a woolen creature exuding class privilege?
Looking through windows to glimpse tits I saw this
instead. It wasn't in the manual. But
applying private cures to collective diseases
occupied every page, it was *The Book of*
the Transparent Tombstone. You could see
all the heroes inside, and downtown Chicago,
men like Mr. Wrigley and buildings like the Tribune
Tower, and what they felt being there like that,
men and buildings squashed inside the look
of a drunk poet chased by wind
like a Sunday supplement on Monday morn.
You could read their desires but not their thoughts,
because you can read these like cigarettes in Lebanon
or Madagascar, and they said,
The thing to be is dead. Complete
thought evacuation. The cold wind
said that. The buildings themselves said
other things, having to do with stubbornness,
heart, commerce, stability, the will
of large men who know the world well
enough to sell it, and when.
You cannot throw up a building in Chicago,
my friend Debra says, and what, say I,
do I look big enough to throw up buildings?
Maybe my steak, but not a whole edifice, no.
You cannot, she says, do that unless it says

something, and buildings in Chicago say
some pretty strange things these days. I look.
They do. They say,
Choke, choke, have another drag,
then take a piss, warm water from the womb,
before starting to fire those tiny letters again.
A deaf woman with sign-language cards lurches
past a horn of plenty filled with writhing pretzels.
The deaf don't get fed here.
Not here now, a waiter tells her, and Gertrude echoes
from the wall:
There is no now now.
In France the dead gods were replaced by waiters
from many parts of the world, many grand waiters, former
czars and dukes and interior ministers
whose manners struck terror into the diners' hearts
and caused a form of socialism whose central burning
question was How do we put the pleasure back in the food?
I call the woman back and say, Ten cards! I have ten
nephews who need to speak your language. They live
in France. They operate a great Deaf Restaurant
where one day the cook chopped a customer's arm off!
On the same spot, a hundred years before
they guillotined a count under the eyes of his pastry
chef! And right now, at this very moment, as I sign,
the half-guillotined bourgeois extends
the stump of his patriotic arm to the former Bulgarian ambassador
(one of the cousins I just mentioned,
also a former Communist and member of the police,
but now a maitre d' and cook, and, secretly, a poet)
who holds it in the air above the slowly turning
rotisserie of history and orates thus:

At the present I cannot address my sentiments to the public,
because they will laugh at them, so I say to myself,
Scribble, scribble in the night, poet.
You are the sole mumbling interpreter of
an older art lost to the anxiety of the milieu,
a man from history, a faucet and a book, in a position
to know and to tell that
culture heroes are not characters, only private heroes are.
And you know also what's inside buildings people don't
really live in, in a country without directories.
But telling the truth after so many years of partisanship
is something I, the ambassador, cannot face.
But a roast, ah, that is incipience *and* fountain!

A very poetic busboy, a cousin I don't remember, streams
out of the kitchen sink
and cuts into the wounded grand bourgeois
and former commissar who keeps a chopping block
covered with parsley jutting from his torso
to keep his selves apart (his
lacerations supple signs of philosophy):

When the great urge to testify came
pushing in like white water from all the rooms
without central heating, and even the railroads,
Monsieur l'Ambassadeur wrapped himself in the blank gaze
of speechless childhood, and was carted off, the coward,
into the virgin pages of a hospital. His revolver
became soft and impotent, and the great hum
of truth that was in the world looking for means
of expression became the generalized din of consumption,
a Berlin wall of televisions, fridges, and stereos
blaring out tears, pent-up sighs, wordless senti-
mentality, and something like physical symptoms,

which the world appeared to be, to him, in him,
and to the watchers. All around him, the cardboard
body of a huge Stalin was growing out of all
proportion to the photographer focusing in on his
tiny head. The editors of night, those antlike
monks in charge of trimming night to reasonable size,
swarmed about the edges of the pulsing heart of cheap
newsprint and tore out long columns of lies where, shattered,
lay the good gossips with their smashed complaints.
Hate-filled stars, asterisks pulsing, literature
called for blood. A stud in hospital slippers,
he moved from switch to switch like a wobbly line
drawn by a drunk engineer around a body dumping ground,
turning off lights, turning on fans, setting off alarms,
tripping over the mad dogs, his colleagues, calling
for certain features of heaven with swollen tongues,
until he found himself before an exalted light pouring
from a stained-glass window, a veritable orgy
of colored light lavished on his puny and emaciated
person, and behind him was a black wood altar containing
an embroidered towel on which something twitched,
a big, great electric fish on a sculpted ceramic dish.
I'd like to be outside, he murmured, but there was
no outside, only this great weight of religion,
this oppression of God, and he looked up. His eyes
rolled upward out of him as effortlessly as if they were
two eggs of brown light lifted by a spring breeze,
lost in the darkness of the Gothic spire's needle
injecting the blue sky with sight. He poured
through his vision, or in his vision, which carried him
like a rickshaw, into the darkness of the tower,
and became a liquid. The liquid that was sight and
presence, which the Great Syringe used, hoping
to get the skies to lift their great empty chambers

where God used to live, and make way for another sky
where He might still reside. And all this with the poor,
bulging, tired eyeballs of a hapless ambassador
from the provinces, who one day, in fear of mortality,
nearly succumbed to the great buzzing bees of truth.
Write this down, it's me, the busboy said.

Aye, but he tells the truth,
the maitre d' he sigh.

Under these circumstances
a little populism is in order,
and the Socialists are just the ones to give it to us,
a little relief for Chrissakes.
Enough of architecture, more planning please!
Indignant, the customer rose to put the bill
into the ballot box, murmuring loud enough for everybody:
Dormir c'est souffler un peu.

Dumb but true, like all things evacuated
by the very truth they claim.
Cryogenics or dogma. Laws or institutions.
Contagion. Pleasure. Violence. Commerce.
The equator. Extravagance. Alaska.
"Just as the glaciers increase," said
F. Nietzsche, our good friend, "when in
the equatorial regions the sun shines upon
the sea with greater force than hitherto,
so may a very strong and spreading spiritualism
be a proof that somewhere or other
the force of feeling has grown most
extraordinarily." So I take a good look
around, and see that brother Nietzsche was
right, as usual. All around us threaded

through the full-time simulation of pleasure
in which the world is presently engaged,
run currents of spuming black arts, the pin-
points of death maps all over them, everything
overlaid with instructions and written in small
print, in filigree, and at certain angles,
and they are shuffled & reshuffled every second
by great paranoid Shakers with both their hands
firmly on the boards and on the flippers.
Come see Commander Monko at the Koinonia,
he's from another dimension, and with him
are a hundred transparent beings eating human
jam with their x-ray hands, and he stands half
in and half out of a large green egg shouting,
What is it? What? Quick! Lie! Stand up! Breathe!
I came here to see how the store is, who minds
the store, one, two, quick, give me your watch,
it's not gold, no good, breathe! One! Two! Quick!
In Seattle the gurus met a few years ago
to discuss the weather. Not good, they said.
Whereupon the volcanoes, and James Merrill, all
erupted, and Edgar Casey bought a piece of Virginia
where winds don't blow, and great shoots of pain & light,
a wire mesh of symbols, slipped like an underquilt
under many parts of speech, including nouns but
mostly adjectives. Which left only the verb people,
us, to shift for ourselves as best we could, dodging
the illusions of the insane mass, and their cabbages,
æsthetics, engineering, and embryos.

Engineers fix up the dried-up mug of the president
with beer. On another billboard
her thighs move slowly to engorge our willing selves.
A pall of sleep lies over us. Occasional violence

wakes up somebody to fun, fucking, fanfare, form,
the full five mintues of total squirming by which
the mess augments and rips things like cloth and materials,
silk and underpants and London Fogs. It's like
a turning upside down of Apollinaire's heart, to spill
all the love on us, coeur renversé, like fairy dust
or cocaine, forever, and with little golden lights in it,
light aphorisms for the abruptly airborne, and the slowly
rising. Dig it here, outside it's all but gone.
Funny how the butterfly Chuang-tzu, a reversible fragment,
insists on the prose of myth and will not,
under any circumstances, recover history for man.
Funny how he and others of angelic ilk get by
both the historical and the ideal, proceeding upward
from this particular man here,
a horny bastard, lost the night entire,
having whiskey, mustard, cocaine, like I said, and great fountains
of words in Blarney's Bar, to the scattered applause
of two fat cops in drag revolving on their stools, over-
sized ballerinas at the Musée Grotesque. These are my
mustard brothers, he proclaims, and these my mustard
sisters, yielders of great big keys fitting the great big
doors of the decades, slammed shut upon the continually
retiring mustard seed of the soul, a firefly, in the dark
tower, with a book and a regret. The book, by Nerval,
flows like the neon above the tired square, nothing
but porn at this hour, and a limp chain or two over sweaty
leather. One can easily see Huncke here, and his Beat
friends, tourists, checking out the night in the interest
of literature, and Soviet critics bent on vodka. But mainly
he enjoys the particular eddy he creates, the swirling
thick mustard of fraternity, and the outside chance
that difference is yet in the world, enormous, if perilous,
and the clashing currents roaming the night may yet

proceed in the direction the twentieth-century *bohème* sketched
out for the collectors and the fools, a direction made
necessary by its being, alas, the only direction not leading
to the Camps and to the Army. Le Paradis n'est pas
artificiel but one must have an alternate hell, or go
with Mr. Lowry to the Farolito, or with Doubleday to
the remainder pit, not to mention Hitler & the rest.
There is no talking that does not lead to this, and to
little plays based on this, and the tap dancer jumped
on the table and made a great dance of this based on
the songs on the radio, eyes closed, feet beating the
Formica with the message that he was here, and he was
glad to be with us, and we were there too. It was a Morse
novel of feet calling and describing all of presence and
its necessity, a beat of forgetting and insistence
on the now, and a firm, albeit desperate, reiteration
of here as being here, I mean there then, here now.
The time has clearly passed for the partisans of now.
If they, we, want to make their, our, presence felt
we have to greatly beat our feet on the ground made
from the heads of our contemporaries filled with
oblivion gas or, worse, detailed visions of exactness,
maps of the very heads they describe *and* fill,
and then hope that the desperate beating in a prose
so beautiful as to wake the lit crit in every heart,
lying (alas!) disconnected from the gas-head at the feet
of some other entities with which we rarely if ever
converse, will reconnect head and heart thus causing
the layer immediately beneath (the great
ontological floor, O Mintho!) to, in its turn, begin
to beat its, their, feet on the heads of those below,
and so on, through all the many cavernlike interiors
of the baby cosmos, until exhausted, intoxicated,
and utterly ecstatic, it meets the Great Outdoors

and their symphonic No. Or Whatever. A real job,
if ever I get one.

The great discovery of my thirties is plurality.
Don't guffaw, Maurice, please listen now.
All my life, and that includes the half of it
which is distinctly literary, soon to surpass in sheer
numbers of years all other, I have thought,
along with babies, bishops, Copernicus, and Sartre,
that one's job in letters and in life
was to express a self attached to a head
which can then be detached, cut off, tu sais.
I tried to stumble my way out of the box of self
as best I could, given the orders I had, which
included complete directions to every museum
on the planet, but found myself creating monads,
perfectly selfish little globes of soap, not firm
like tits, nor smooth like spheres, horrid new
selves bent on conquering the gas stations for new
energy to propagate themselves concentrically
through life and lit and sometimes through the park.
Which is not, as I see it now, the point.
The point—put here your place names with Point—
is Plurality, Point Plurality, to be exact,
a landmark that's been here all along, on which
Mr. Jefferson grounded us and made us a building
at Monticello, in Virginia. Point Plurality, almost
exactly the way it is in Mr. Murdoch's papers,
and in these buildings from the days before
taxes, modesty, civic restraint and fake humility,
and the way all noble rhetoric would have it,
including my citizenship lecture and the loving
drunken bash afterward, in other forms. In other
words, all other words, not just the tolerance

of difference, but the joyful welcoming of differences
into one's heart spread out like the pages
of a newspaper. The pursuit of the dialectic,
as Monsieur l'Ambassadeur would say, without which
one cannot live, although, alas, it is much harder
to practice in words than in the kitchen.

For you, I said.

He handed me back my arm.
Whereupon I grasped tightly my cliché and thin-lipped,
went through the door into the street
where the small animals are barbecued.
I did enjoy the pale winter sun.
I made the most of the spring breeze that lifted minis.
I let my tongue wag into the summer heat and collected
a whole urn full of lovely sweat.
In the fall I fell with the leaves and was *désuet*.
Winter came to take me to bed.
Streets, cities, waiters, and parades—
these were the hair my various barbers chopped,
falling in great profusion into place, exactly
where they belonged or not. So using the conveyance
of the "I" to get us through the streets, I came
to the exact meeting place of a thousand "I"s
clamoring for attention with an uninterrupted
belief in culture and the Pie.
I hovered there until I found you.

It was no ordinary party. Ted Berrigan was there.
Anselm too. And so were all the great orators of
our time and theirs, and a number of philosophers
in the corners, with that corned-beef look in their
deli eyes. And the music was L O U D! I mean,

we rocked! But for all that, you could hear
every word and our voices were nearly alien
to us because that unnaturally low or high pitch that
we acquired in order to talk above or below music
was nearly gone, and we spoke the way people spoke
for thousands of years, without the din
of perceptual cultural imperialism, but clearly
in the din of the market only, if we so choose.
I mean, when we wanted din we went to the market
and talked so the policeman wouldn't hear us.
The world is louder but the policemen listen better.
The old chickens squawking and the screaming gypsies
were as good as nature when we needed cover.
Like I say, we were both loud and clear
and happy knowing both schedules and eternity,
simultaneously upside down and horizontal
like bars on a music sheet in a big bed!
But there were some gents and gentians on the canopies
who looked as if they'd eaten the green apples of jealousy
and then OD'd on the wormy peaches of reason,
embarrassed recipients of large grants and prizes who
had removed themselves from human company.
One of these, a pathetic necrophiliac with spindly legs,
said that when the mind matures the sentences
come fully fleshed, in erect glory, and indeed
a full-fleshed sentence hung at half-mast from his sad
erection. It was *I paid for the gas so where am I?*
There are these bummers even in heaven, close even
to the mystery itself, not too close, of course, for
fear of being burned, but close enough. They sit or lounge
within sight of the mystery itself, scribbling on, not
seeing it. Once in a while they stop dead in their tracks
and wriggle as if the devil was in them. What happens is
that the mystery has a public-address system and it broadcasts

spontaneously and for fun, to blow their minds.
The mystery with built-in megaphone came thus to Lorca,
Mayakovski, Hikmet, and Ritsos, but not in translation.
Most times, however, the mystery whispers, depending
on attention for its erotic food, which it demands
without fail, to keep its flames fanned. "Our job," said
brother Blaga, "is not to uncover it but to increase
its mysteriousness." And so the mystery burns
giving off only enough light for the enormous job
of making oneself. Each time, every night, all
experience must be renewed. Others' successes or
failures are of no importance. The flames are not
bookish, and the sooner you give a child his or her wings
the sooner they'll get on with it, and that is how
from generation to generation the overprotected rich
get weaker, and overprotective tribes lose their sense
of hearing and their anger, and they begin to cater
to the dead. The dead lie like a heavy book cover
on us, our tombstone. It is their business to take
our time, to oppress us as much as they can, until
we say everything for them and train others to be dead.
They blackmail us every minute, so fuck them!
Must we always, like mad Swiss bankers, synchronize
what happened *then* to what happens *now?*
I'll write the poetry I always wanted to, or none at all.
The conventions of my generation, life, teachers,
lovers, maps, cars, music, art, the things I've said,
fuck 'em all, ploys clearly of the anxious dead!
The content that fills the flowing shapes
of my heart's pure yearning is communal like the city.
A fraudulent but real place like any other.
The infinite and the political do not exclude each other.
The particulars of a face need not break the concentration
of desire. Au contraire, they could augment it. And

in psychoanalysis and other therapies, people pay
for what they are missing, but not in order to recover it,
only to be confirmed in their lack, to be reassured
of the normality of absence, of the utter popularity of
the abyss, the sanctioned nothingness, the triviality
of death. "Oh, we were vacated by the gods," they cry,
"so we had to put language in the hole! Or waiters!"
Well, I prefer the mask to the well-thought nothingness,
as I have said before, and I only took this job because
no one is doing it. The job always, the only job,
is to be an ontological reminder, a real pain in the
ass, reminding everyone why we took up the pen
in the first place, to scratch ourselves on the wall
or under the aching arm, to kick open the lid, to set
the water free, the hair loose, the spirit flowing.
Make you hear again that metarooster crowing!

After I had my soup, a fat lobbyist, selling satellite
contracts to Indian and African businessmen at the next
table, took football jackets out of his satchel
and presented them to the grateful foreign nationals
who interrupted their scheming on how to get their
countries' treasuries to Switzerland, for a minute,
and said, "The Raiders! Yeah! Yeah! We love the Raiders!"
I interrupted my meditation and thought of Salvador
Dali, how it is possible to praise this world and
plunder it, without renouncing either others or the next.
I also gave a brief thought, because my curry was late,
to Kant's disciple Fichte, who said, "The Not-I is the
product of the I," a truly egocentric take needing
an instant Galileo. On the other hand, and here
I fiddled with my spoon, without the consciousness
illuminating the big It out there, how are we to see
it? By the neon of Chicago, natch! And then

the curry came, and it was hot, a red mountain atop
a purely golden bed of rice surrounded by little opal-green
islands of onion and mango chutney, and warm hissing
flat breads giving off air bubbles, and hope. The I
is neither product nor originator of the Not-I. That is
posing the problem falsely. The I is the enemy of
the Not-I, its colonizer, conqueror, and exploiter,
and here I dove into my food and was fierily gone.
The I is in the business of substance sucking, de-
sacralizing all the routes and getting fat.
The Unknown is my food, and that is that. I take
my rest at the Richmont Hotel and have my hair
groomed, and then I walk. There are
people who wish to show their solidarity with their
fellow creatures. Others want only to display
a spiritual difference. My company is with
the former but my sympathies with the latter. After
the light comes the odd turn, then the giant feather.
In the warm lobby I find the latest newspapers. I sigh
for Carmen at the cinema. Oh, close my word-weary mouth,
you arch, cross, vaulted, fleeing Gypsy slut!

BELLIGERENCE

INTRODUCTION

• *Belligerence*
Minneapolis: Coffee House Press, 1991 (Editor, Allan Kornblum)

The Francesco Clemente cover says it all: a wide-eyed man thoughtfully and disbelievingly considers things, while above or behind him a man and a woman are locked in a faceless embrace. In 1989, the regime of Nicolae Ceaușescu was violently overthrown as the last red domino of Soviet empire fell. I reported it live on NPR and ABC news. I made a film, "Road Scholar" (1991), a travel documentary where I drove across America in a red Cadillac convertible, looking at small utopian communities to see how they fared after the demise of state communism. The movie, directed by Roger Weisberg and Jean de Segonzac, won a Peabody Award, but I was in the midst of emotional upheaval. The world had gone from a seemingly eternal black and white, bipolar stability, to an uncertain fragmentation that I felt in my own self. The next few poetry books, beginning with this, are engaged with the world of politics and technology as much as my shifting interior terrain.

belligerence

In the irruptive mode
I wear no hat
& hate what I see
in the rearview mirror
except silver balls.
When I was all the rage
I was in disruptive mode
& wore the instructions
on my Reeboks to a frazzle
between the lines of what
everybody read and the high-
way stripes painted there.
Actually shoes in those days
had no names but I was a futurist.
Mealtimes at Hojo's & Wendy's—
the plastic tablecloths
had squares in them
and the prices were cheap
obsessively and people
in those days laughed
until their faces
became tic-tac-toe boards
& few could tell death to shut up,
Life was no fucking (pre)text.
Menus with everything under one
dollar were not unknown.
Anyway, only the greatest
could write it down. I was

among them. Since then, volcanoes
have been miniaturized,
everyone gets to be
a little sick. I know
everyone who works here,
they are not happy,
I wear a dunce cap.

another globe

Nel mezzo del camino I found myself
in the middle class
looking at two diverging options:
ideology and addiction.
My triumph is to practice both.
Revirginate or Perish!
Learn how to read to trees!
(You never know who might be listening
when the class enemy is in the class.)
Can he be that hombre
who walks into town
followed by a slow caravan
of Toyota vans laden
with empty mail sacks
ready to buy everything?
The shelves, the things on them,
the stores themselves,
the clerks' personal effects,
watches, homes, mothers?
And gives them
whatever they ask for?
When this hombre leaves,
the town wobbles like a great
plucked chicken
and shivers from cheap wind.
This hombre then sits
in on a card game
west of the Pecos

and tells this joke
to the members of the Cabinet:
An old Jew asks the Soviet
border guards for a globe
to see where he should go.
After hours of careful study
he returns it & asks:
Do you have another globe?
In the end we remember not the joke
nor the out-of-place place where
he tells it to the people
but the fact that we all detest living
through the adroit manipulations
of the small-print clauses
of our social contract.
Therefore you in the front row
wouldn't you rather
Do It Your Way?
Don Juan, narcissist
whose job is to upset order
and the authority spent
establishing it,
releases energy
teased into being
by his hat.
Once a man loses his taste for himself
he becomes completely unsavory: meat
spoils from within.
Others seep in through the chinks
and chomp chomp their way through heart & gut.
Two careless lovers are worth one thousand bankers.
The world is froth over the surface
of an untouched hard core
that first looks real,

then nostalgic, then Betamax.
I stagger from BBQ to BBQ
& never see sobriety anymore.

leaves of nerves

Nylon is a wonderful thing in a city with trees.
Inside the wilderness of self
is outside but outside
is still inside
for Mr. Smith from St. Louis
who phones
to say all night I was inside
his head. "I was hoping
to speak to your message machine."
These are the very rich hours
of the Middle-Aged Duc of Poesy.
Onward & beyond
to the times when one would like
to write through
the machinery,
namely the love current,
but how much one belongs in the world
depends on how brightly
one talks to the police.
The aggression of health is badly understood.

demands of exile
for Dorin Tudoran

We are growing a bitter seed issue
of poets who can't go home again.
Here squat men in fat suits papillon greasy
huddle in dark Chicago basements
perched on writing tables to leap
to Paris into Biedermeier inkstands.
Prettiness of course isn't the issue
when one has left behind all the pretty
things and is now at the mercy of scents,
happenstance, emigration, digestion.
Nor is the issue courage or top form
though both are necessary in order
to play sweep over the borders of official
form that need be completed and punctuated.
Not nostalgia not horror not righteousness
though in various degrees these are the alarm
clock perched on the wobbly armoire, child
of one Eternity and an enraged grownup
who saw Her bathing one day at the non-
political shore of childhood and caused
them to merge into a murderous
infinity whose issue is fiery death
and more death. For now they are kept apart
by the writing hand. The pen prevents
the closing of the fist and prices being
what they are it's a good thing too.
Not indignation, intelligence, rage,

though in various bourgeois measure
these too once mixed well to steer
the hornet nest of culture, causing bees
to rise from pamphlets into better print.
Home is a car on the road to a cottage
filled with storytelling mythmaking rustics
leaning on a future composed of woven pelts,
miles of sausages, milk and approximate figures
which form the antihistorical peak
where one rests in the company
of national fiction at its most formal ease
under a sky of homespun ambiguities and goat.
No those are not the issues though each line
makes the jar buzz and sets the fashion free.
The issue is ease, and when. The bitterness
thereof is the lack of it, the Sunday
afternoon going to bad movies
made by people one knows slightly,
then letting the haze of a cigarette
over Turkish coffee push the country
forward, a miraculous machine
that is the opposite of a cement truck.

intention

for Tom Clark

Poems be not intended
therefore I be always writin
never intendin

"Wake up/ have coffee/
write a poem/ what else/
is there?" (Elinor Nauen)

Wake up/ have coffee/ puzzle
dream/ about attention:
partial, full & deep./ Attention
paths/ are fascicles./ They work
negatively./ We engage only
inattention./ So go back/
to sleep/ dream some more/
about doors./ There is

the temptation to sprinkle
quotation marks about
(and slashing 'em)
in that sense, intention
abounds to make legit
the sense in which attention
could be intentional.

My intention is to make a poem
that includes all the great
lines ever written;

I intend this poem to be here
long after you've gone.

It was my intention to present
you with something
leading to sex. I intended
to apologize for the other night
with this humble poem
which has nothing to do with it.

I intend to sue you for character
defamation, let this poem serve
as a pre-subpoena. Intentionally,
I leave these little scratches
on your desk, I made them in a dream.

Intent upon my feelings I came
upon these words: I was full of good
intentions until I saw what I'd wrought
and swore to nevermore complain. Ill
intentions got me here with the ill
wind of the age filling the sails
of my poem: I'll make you something
on purpose to offset being lost.

It was the intention of all present
to palliate loss with literature:
it all came to naught when our leader
folded up the tent of his splendid
intentions, mounted anybody's steed,
took off in an uncertain direction.

What is found depends entirely
on being lost.

The failure of internationalism
is due in part to its containing
intention; likewise intonation,
internation, installation.

We knew exactly where to install
beauty but the electrical codes
are a century old, so we had
to start from scratch with noble
intentions but not much
enthusiasm, which doomed us.

Furthermore, there is enough
intention in language
to sink any would-be orator
so why give a headache to yourself,
you are a mess of botched intentions
as it is, Harry?

We considered the proposition
that the body might be
a superbly intentional
cooperative farmed out
to a cosmic purpose
and that the poem in its
organicity might be more
like the body than any-
thing less organized
and came to rest upon
the thought that the poem
as a body has no
choice, there being little
in nature or in art that
isn't organized instantly

upon expression. To make
is to order which is why
it is important to make
without a plan. Intention
lands one in bed with cliché,
which is somebody's old plan
to bed somebody else's old
plan—Don Juan's intentions

were from the beginning
to seduce the good ladies
of Seville though he had most
rudimentary ideas on how
to proceed, having only
an attitude and not a system.

Attitude differs from intention.
It is the Ur-ground of action
before the plan. Yes, I have
an attitude but it's no plan,
mother, I just want to set sail
for parts unknown, and later
when we recall the journey
for our homebound friends
we'll invent a whole new journey
we will never have unless we leave
right now. Forget the telling.

I never intended to get around
the two things that smack of intention,
the two forbidden rocks upon whose flanks
many a traveler cracked and died,
postintention and autograph.

Long after the journey's done
the postintentional revisionist
plunges his Soviet pen into the facts
and spaces them intentionally
to make visible the line
on which flutter the bloody rags
of certain swollen egos.
I have done this, and I'm not proud.

Likewise the autograph by being
set before the journey like the word
journey before mounting,
pollutes the very journey with intention.
Of this I have been also guilty.

Forgive us our intentions, dear reader,
they were only attitudes gone flatter.

christmas in new york
for Laura

Trees torpedoes Soviet galoshes
books violins woolen socks
Mexico Argentina Korea Peru.
We promenade in steamy human corn.
An actress with her arm wrapped
around gift-wrapped mannequin
calls mom in snowbound Arkansas.
People people the island
wrapped around each other
lit scroll-like Chinese on
Chinatown marquee
where we suck duck feet
that once walked the sturdy earth.
Oh tender feet whose flesh we sweetly suck!
The string on our hearts is nigh undone.
Ghosts nine feet tall come bounding through the slush!
We are so nicely dressed!
Parcels with wings in ghostly disarray
argue with their lost souls in traffic
gifts exchanged desperately fast!
We tangle ourselves to wind-whipped
humanity blowing about the future
when our children will have nice toys.
The world has a million elbows
resting on fine tables in the bistro de la vida.
All exchange is slush balderdash
O great haberdasher!

O pure metal money.
O truth under duress—this being
that time—there are no words
that are not for sale. Yet we know:
outside the body begins the lie.
Outside that the newspaper.
And the bum wrapped in it
will not change tomorrow's news
though tomorrow both paper and body
will be a white mound of snow,
an unsystematic library, confusion
of what lived and what died
before it could be re-read
or how from inside ourselves
the big snow came
to invade with beauty
so recently rent a world.
The magic lounges wrapped
in jukebox steam
give good detail to whatever makes it in.
O baby, call in the the surface-to-air messenger,
the caffeinated pigeon
with the beating of his trained
telegraph across the années.
O differentiated lumps of amore!
O garbage dump masses having us for dinner
you on a platter me on a cloud!
Food for everybody.
L'âme de Madame is now served.
Erectile tissue paper in crêpe de chine
rose-pinks to burst its mauve bows.
Death to the military metaphors:
sentences, captains, bullets, reports.
Without a roof we revel in being,

wrapped for others—keepsakes
of a state and time when
human beings are:

1) rubber animals who bend well and far
        held tightly between frozen mitts

2) empty drawing on swirling imagoes to make credible thickness
        i.e., belabored snowmen and snowwomen

3) impressions on Japanese screen

4) comic algebra

5) excess food covered by tweed

6) mute newlyweds wrapped in a single fur

7) baby mimes doing stuff with their toes

8) company representatives (the Trans-
        Siberian Railroad, the Alaska goldrush)

9) travel dust from luminous hair
        of aliens with cuneiform legs
dancing the poignant resiliency of almost anything

10) hardy gossamer.

The juke pivots in the end-century
for Genghis wherever he is,
and Elvis Kahn, tailor to history,
in Jersey over the smoke where he
cuts the falling snow to fit

everyone so they'll look sublime:
newts en masque, popes en croûte,
flares on restaurant tables
where the dons of beauty &
donnas of grace pose
in the unfathomable
instrumentation of seated self.
The Dream of Perfection neatly fits
the Dream of Wickedness about the waist
of the Dream of Power 'round the testes
of the Dream of Transformation.
Above the wingèd tedium
of phones ringing in Christmas splendor
the party calls us to the source
of the objective world
whose diamond opens briefly
like a disco at some pink odd point
where commerce ceases and exchange begins
& dreaming well accoutred
in pleasure and so dry.

a leafy angel

to the Columms Hotel

Quietly at the corner table
where the dry fountain
drowns in unswept leaves
under its disconsolate angel,
the slim boy in the shadow
of the blooming jeune fille
has opened Postmodern Art,
a book. Twixt happiness
and unhappiness
the only break we get
she thinks is sleep.
Certain mental interiors
exist only in French
is what he thinks.
Stranger still she is chief thespian
in a play
taking place presently in her mind
where she does bad things
in order to build capital
for masturbation
with a visiting European
on whose shoulders
run little trains
powered by oblivion.
At the streetcar stop
an old woman in mourning black
watches her younger self run

alongside a mostly naked runner
following the streetcar line
to a perfect body.
They are Jasmine and Sweet Olive,
they have just met
in 1924 in The City
That Lives for Its Belles,
a bar.
Stranger sit quietly here
this evening
at the Columns Hotel
on the terrace at dusk
where light goes out with flair
on froufrou and history.
Outside the body, happily,
begins the lie.

IT WAS TODAY

INTRODUCTION

- *It Was Today*
  Minneapolis: Coffee House Press, 2003 (editor, Allan Kornbum)

Indeed it was. I lived in New Orleans, taught in Baton Rouge, lived with passion and traveled with a vengeance. America was rolling in money, the stock market was booming, the internet exploded to change irrevocably how humans did business in the world. The "end of history" appeared to coincide with the glass house of technology we were all going to live in, and possibilities looked endless to everyone, except poets, of course, who make a point of walking the opposite way from the crowd. Even so, it was hard to keep from being swept away by the wave of what a financial poet called "irrational exuberance." In midst of this orgy, the wise voices of two Chinese poets from the fourteenth century started calling insistently to me: Lu Li, a courtesan at the imperial court, and Weng Li, a soldier. Their time was brutal and primitive, but their joys were eternal. They were new personae, the first in a long time, and their purpose seemed to be a warning, a caveat from history.

LU LI AND WENG LI

Lu Li and Weng Li lived in China in the Mongol Century (1279-1368). Lu Li was a courtesan at the imperial court, Weng Li was a warrior. They were either brother and sister or lovers or, perhaps, both. They wrote poems for each other without any certainty that the other would ever read them. All we know about them comes from their poems. After the manuscript, carefully bound together as if someone was preparing it for publication, was found in 1989, two more years passed before a modern Chinese translation by Wang Shih appeared. The first translation in the West was into Portuguese by Dr. Alberto S. Figueroa from the University of Lisbon. This superb translation by Len Darien is from both the Chinese and the Portuguese. After publication, there was a wave of interest in these late thirteenth-century poets, and translation into Romanian, German, and French followed. A Chinese scholar, unable to find the Chinese translation in China, questioned their authenticity. "These poets," he wrote, "are entirely too modern. They speak across the ages clearer than most of us speak across the room." But this is precisely what poetry, from whatever age, does. Nonetheless, a wave of scholarly skepticism followed the Beijing professor's article. Faced with this near-universal distraction, Len Darien, the translator, admitted that there was no Chinese version, and that, in fact, there was no Len Darien. Len Darien was a nom-de-plume for the editor of *Exquisite Corpse*, who was indeed writing his poems from across the room to his muse Laura, who helped give form to Lu Li's voice while Weng warred. Both Lu Li and Weng Li eventually took possession of Andrei Codrescu, who faithfully wrote down what they said. Lu Li and Weng Li are not a literary hoax. Granted, they arrived in English in an unconventional way, but they are here, regardless.

LU LI

lying on my back
the emperor's astrologer on top of me
I thought of the stars
years ago they foretold this
but the astrologers could not tell
that their labors were in vain
even the stars have no say
in who works for them

*

the emperor's waiting rooms
reek of perfume
I can tell who has visited here
their scents are stacked like paper
in the imperial library
they are all greedy and fearful
I like the market better
the sweat of humans and horses
fears no one there

*

I did not feel like being dressed today
I sent away my maid
I made a hill of my clothes
in the middle of the floor
the wind rattled the shutters
all day

I am no one without my clothes
I could have stayed like that forever
In the evening a messenger came
I stepped into my clothes
and was Lu Li again

*

ten red beans
ten white beans
a black stone
ten times in a day
I moved them
no one else
can play my game
the cook surprised me
one of them I said
will make a meal
for the whole palace
she smiled knowingly
her hair was white

*

the sweet-smelling one
left at dawn
a rainy day
he is going to translate
indian poetry
for our emperor
whose mind is far away from war
my beloved Weng Li
makes war far away

*

my friend's jade comb
looks better in my hair
the man who gave it to her
sleeps better on my pillow

*

I lie down
for a moment
clouds pass
summer is beginning
I think I will visit
my parents
in the country

*

the emperor has a red monkey
he strokes it so much it is bald
his sleeve always holds seeds
for his singing birds
he can only sleep on the fur
of a bear he killed in his youth
he is like a woman who chews
red beetles all day
or like Lu Li who sits on her step
outside her room rubbing smooth
her pretty stones
the empire is built of empty gestures
somewhere Weng sheds blood for it
on hillsides bald as the emperor's monkey

*

today was rainy
the palace was shrouded
I lost my way to the bath
the women laughed
here comes Lu Li already wet
they played with me
a bursting cloud

*

I slapped little Chen
for braiding my hair too roughly
she is only twelve
her mind is already elsewhere
she thinks of her own hair
all day long she looks past me in the mirror
she is my mirror I was once like her
my lady slapped me too
we women descend through the ages
on a ladder of hair
each one looks up in the mirror
of the one above her

*

the captain of the guards
the chief notary and
the tax collector
for the whole empire
were beheaded today
everyone rejoiced
at the market the women
gave rice cakes free
everyone shouted

the emperor is just
the hard men are gone
let them rejoice this day
new men are coming
to work at dawn

WENG LI

the village henchman
poisoned the well
threw himself in it
for good measure
everyone else fled
we set fire to the empty sheds
we were thirsty for water
not for blood
that night I heard
laughter from the well
next day we rode far

*

the snow fell all night
when I stepped out of my tent
the beards of old men
had wrapped everything
wisdom has come to us I thought
I heard a white mound groan
and another grunt
and one farted loudly
the snow is kind
but wisdom is far away

*

on a lone tree in a clearing
autumn left an apple

it is wrinkled and stubborn
an old whore's behind
everyone wants to eat it
no one wants the others to see him
the emperor's best men
are afraid of an apple
the shame will make us kill
more people tomorrow

*

there was no one on the street to greet us
the houses were on fire
we torched them all
a stubborn old man
sat on an old tree stump
in front of his blazing pigsty
singing a song to himself
I tipped my lance to him
he did not see me

*

the village headman presented our lord
with two jade lovers
we passed them from hand to hand
each man thought of his loved one
when the figures were returned
the jade was dark
so many lovers

*

tonight our cook
found only a small dog
the broth was thin
the star in the sky
some call the Dog
filled our empty bowls

*

treason was twice punished today
a horseman was halved by sword
his foot soldier was torn to pieces
tied to four horses
from the hills the enemy watched
today we meet in the field
my lord and I drank silently all night

*

they tell a story
about a country
where no one could read
the monks there
are unafraid
no one can see
what he writes of them

*

the philosophers quarrel
about how the world was made
some say the stars made us
others say the gods did
I take no part in their discussions

I watch a boy watch a girl
the grass whispers when they pass

*

seven times in one year
I have written Lu Li
not once did she answer
seven times she read
every letter
she knows them by heart

*

I have served under seven lords
some were generous with their gold
I like my horse best of all
we have ridden so far from home
he sometimes looks at me
I know that he remembers

*

I have no use
for the village I conquered
for my lord
the big house in the middle
of the town
looks at me
through the eyes of a young girl

*

when I am killed
my fellow soldiers
will find my poetry
under my saddle
they will laugh
they will say
all this time
we thought he was like us

*

a tower
made of bricks
must be seen
with eyes of steel
this is how men
of war think
the tower
of words
I am making
should be seen
with velvet eyes
those are not the eyes
of anyone here
I have to look
in the night sky
for those eyes

*

where there were dragons
cities will spring up
the storyteller said
he was polished

a speaking walnut
we had killed
all the dragons
but only he could see
the cities
I listened
to his stories
I did not care to see
those cities

Coda

the emperor's ears
are grown weary of the phone
they have heard many causes
he had no idea Lu Li
had a cause
Lu Li he always thought
just was
and would always be
now the telephone
and the television
have warped her mind
one with its ring
the other with its models
of how life should be
next thing you'll know
I'm not the emperor
and you're not Lu Li
now only asses would think
such a thing is better

nickelodeon

have 20th century
hangover in change
jars good american
change while paper
in denominations
of one million per
square toilet roll
fills the empty
dreams of romanians
with numbers not much
else certainly not
sausages on a grill
with new wine in love
in let's say 1965
when nothing not even
communism could stop
the sap from overcoming
the ballyhooed and now
forgotten curtain
I had a youth once
I was very good at it

to poetry

that nervous energy
is called poetry
when you can't stand
either still or the world
it's that groove
even half asleep
because the pharmacy
of control the chemical
frame around the window
of liberty is stealing
away half the energy
even then the nervous
half-asleep energy
is still poetry
in full bloom
the window open
you crawl through
to get to the bar
and to the girls
is really open to poetry
so this year go there

the portuguese eat a dish

called feijoada
heavy with beans
cabbages potatoes ham
kale roasted manioc
orange slices on top
the jews eat a similar
dish sans ham
called cholent
they took it with them
to brazil every saturday
on one side of the street
the jews eat their beans
while on the other
the maranos eat theirs
brazil said the poet machado
is sometimes a hambone

old snake ponders

Heavens! What symptoms are these? Unrelenting
Synchronicity followed by sheer idiocy why me?
The serpent swallows his tail or is about to and is
Amazed to find how much older his tail has gotten
But even as he swallows he is not without hope of
Finding his old tail the delyumicious young tail
He used to chew on for hours when he was bored
In class This just can't be the same tail so maybe
He shouldn't swallow it even though he's in a
Swallowing tail kind of mood and he knows only
Too well that there is no more snake afterward
So this must be a cosmic joke set up by his dead
Friends either that or this kind of thing in subtler
Forms goes on all the time and snakes everywhere
Disappear routinely under the pressure
Of synchronicity What makes him such a special snake?
And the sheer idiocy is there to exhaust him
Long enough to consider such matters O snake
You are long silly belt-like greedy and stupid!

my name is andrei codrescu
for tristan

My first book of poetry was called *License to Carry a Gun*.
It was written in 1968.
1968 was the year when guns took down
Martin Luther King and Robert Kennedy.
The title of my book meant that in a crazy time
one had to be crazier
and that meant not just having a gun
but BEING a gun.
Later that year at a poetry reading
a group of us "shot" some boring poets
with fake guns while shouting
"Death to Bourgeois Poetry!"
and after the poetry reading
I was busted by two plainclothes policemen
who said I had just robbed a store
with my fake gun
and later that year
I got held up at gunpoint.
And later yet
in August of 1996
Jonathan Ferrara handed me a twisted machine-pistol
at a poetry reading
(there were only a few boring bourgeois poets there)
and told me to make art out of it
and I gave the gun to my son to hold
without telling him that I was supposed to make
art out of it

and he put it in his backpack
and later yet
he dropped it in a garbage can
on his way home.
This is why there is no gun here
only a poem.
And when I said to my son: shit,
what am I gonna do with no gun?
he said: You made enough art
out of guns already.
Let this one pass.

my son came over

my son and I
said I didn't
want to see no
thracian charm
bracelets to read
the mysterious
inscriptions on them
though the dacians
were the ancestors
of romanians and I
might have by some
metempsychotic
process deciphered
them and no I said
I didn't want
to paddle for an hour
on the lake in city
park but I might
want to take up
a sport sometime
and we went through
all the sports I
might take up and I
decided against tennis
handball racquetball
or running because they
kill guys my age
just this year my friend

tom dent died playing
tennis and maybe I
wanted to swim and my son
said that you can play
all sports relaxed and I
said let's play chess
and when we came
to my place I said
not today maybe some
other time I
am a horrid and cranky
old man but my son
said sweetly some other
time so tomorrow
we will translate poems
from the spanish they
are about how hard
the world is and I
think that they are also
about mean old men but I
hope that they are about joy

as tears go by

I want to cry whenever I hear Marianne Faithfull sing "As Tears Go By" because she's watching children play and children always make me cry because I think that it's a big bad world that's mean to children. It was mean to me, certainly, when I was a child. I cried when my mother left me with my grandmother. I cried when my grandmother left me at school. I cried when my father left the country—and us— forever. I cried when Stalin died.

I cried when my mother cried. And that was often. Her tears were both specific and generic. They were specific when it was a matter of a man leaving her. They were generic when she cried because life and the world were unbearable. And sometimes she cried neither specifically nor generically but deeper like an animal. And those were not her tears, they were the tears of unfairness for being a woman, for being a Jew, for being punished for something she didn't know the name of. I sometimes cried with her like that and those tears just flowed through us on their way somewhere else: they were part of a river of tears that runs through our kind since the beginning of time. This river sweeps us all in its swell and we stand in it keening, wailing, and arguing with something invisible in the language of lamentations. My mother's two aunts, my grandmother's sisters, who died at Auschwitz, were swept away by this river.

I rarely cry now. Sometimes I'm filled by love or sorrow and I feel the tears rising—but I usually check them. I did cry when Romania overthrew the Ceaușescu dictatorship. Prematurely, perhaps. I'm afraid that if I start crying I'll never stop. Not for any particular, or even generic reason. But for that animal reason that leads to the river of tears.

In Romanian folktales the tears of young girls become flowers. But what happens to the tears of aging poets? They become sharpened spikes, rusted bollards, fish hooks, spears, barbed wire. . . . Their tears are bitter! Keep the poets from crying!

often after a public event

a pretty girl curly black hair
framing literary ambition
or a shy tall boy black curly
hair burning with sympathy

will say something in a foreign
accent to me we are from bosnia
hungarians or jews my mother
was born near your city back then
it was in another country

now we are from here what should
we do with our accents

do like me I say
keep talking

brâncuși's fish

it is 1930
& fish bird and turtle
have taken the center stage
explaining Constantin
to the world:
left Romania
like a turtle
with an apocryphal barrel
on my back full of student
works & arrived in Paris
the night a great party at Picabia's
stood still for a moment;
flew bird-like into the new century
of airplanes and transatlantic
commerce; the Americans
wanted to understand flight
they were born to it
they wanted to know its art
but above all I loved
the sonorous silence
of the dark bodies
of the women of the new century
who were not afraid to swim
in the dark with me and come up
only now and then for a mouthful
of brandy and champagne
& who loved the stealth
of abstracting all that jumble

of objects that cluttered everything
in the cubists' pads & were made
worse by the surrealists
with their mania for measurements
& advertising; Mina Loy
who was struck by the kinesthetic
purity of my bronze bird
& Nancy Cunard whose fabled ships
were a fish fable, & Peggy Peggy,
of course Peggy & we swam before
& after my famous cabbage rolls
in the metaphysical whiteness
of the year 1930:
every year since & every decade
is turtle bird or fish
in 1989 my bird soared again
then labored the turtle on
its laborious climb
then comes again the fish.
things look up & away.
time, show us how you swim

the revolution and the poet

bucharest january 1, 1990

The poet needs revolution every decade
like the wounded need transfusions.
There is still blood on the snow in Bucharest.
The people with flags unfurled atop tanks
strike the perfect revolutionary poses
the tableaux vivants of years of Marxist
schooling. The French fall in love with them.
This is the snow sprung live from every
painting between 1846–1965 and sculpture, too:
the bronze train atop of which Lenin arrives
at the Finland station
where two lovers have found a dark place for love.
Only now Lenin is down and the lovers are on top.
This is the new decade in Bucharest, snowy New Year
by the blazing candles of the martyrs' shrine
drunk with the millennium
schooling complete at last

in jerusalem on my 48th birthday

My mustache is all that remains of Stalin.
At the tomb of Jesus the miracles surround us.
Sister Rodica knows every single one of them.
The stone of Golgotha is cracked under us.
The blood of the Crucified washed the skull of Adam.
The candles of believers at Easter light from the Light.
The Light hovers before it bursts into flames.
In that hovering the sick are healed.
Not one but many icons cry and ooze myrrh.
Especially the Mother of God whose Doloroso Mementos
fill Jerusalem with womanly lament.
Endlessly the stones crack when God and His are hurt.
And the Wailing Wall waits for us and it heats us up
in the rain. We put our wet heads against it
and against all the soggy paper prayers in it.
A young rabbi reads a prayer for health. Hand him
twenty shekels. Across the wall on a ridge a solid
mass of black-clad faithful stands under a banner
welcoming the Messiah. A donkey laden
with gasoline cans descends to the Via Dolorosa.
Two horses have broken free & are running into traffic.
The Mount of Olives' olive trees look scrawny.
Scrawny they look in the Garden of Gethsemane!
And the young Arabs look at us with burning eyes.
And young Israelis with machine guns measure everyone.
The spot where the Mother of God fainted.
The house of the Last Supper.
The church over the spot where Simon Peter heard the rooster crow.

The tombs of the patriarchs.
The lion of David over the Damascus Gate.
The son of David Absalom in his grave.
The kings and the prophets of Israel in their graves.
The Golden Gate built by the Turks to stop the endless
comings of too many Messiahs.
City of Messiahs on my birthday.
From grave to grave in Israel.
My father's. The million and a half
children's flickering candle-lit souls in an infinity
of mirrors at Vad Yashem, Benny Hendel's voice
reading out some of them.
The tomb of Jesus.
The Wailing Wall.
Wall to wall graves, O Jerusalem.
The grave of old worlds, new worlds, future worlds.
Grave waiting for graves.
This is where I celebrate my birth 48 years ago,
everything either beginning in 1946 or 1948.
The German Transylvanian Hospice St. Charles
next to the walled-in Templars' Cemetery.
Knots of forty-sixes and forty-eights.
Miri once saw an enormous coffin go in the gate.
Full of the Templars' treasure, including the Holy Grail.
The Romanian Church at 46 Shiftei Israel.
And all around, Israel, a country of children
milling about the streets while the elder minority
eat cakes and debate the world around coffee tables
but mainly debate the Jews because to Jews
the most fascinating thing in the world is Jews.
"Can you believe a whole country full of Jews?" asks Benny.
It was the letters that got me, I say, the Hebrew letters
that always, for me, were a bit mysterious and forbidden.
And we remember the Haifa oranges of our Romanian childhood,

mysterious globes of gold wrapped in crinkly tissue,
black Jewish letters burning on it like midnight fires
in the waning late hours of Stalinism.
And in this late age of computers the Jews await the Messiah
and Christians are ready for the End Times and the Second Coming
and writers lament the end of the book
and the Dead Sea scrolls say many circular things
in the Torah-like scroll at the Israel Museum,
an apple core at the center of Jewish insecurity.
The bazaar throbs with spices and cassette tapes.
The muezzin calls from his tower. The beating of the clapper
against the bell is the sound of nails driven into our Savior.
Thank you, Sister Rodica. And you know what else,
Paradise was closed to men until the Ascension of Christ.
And then it opened and now all men and women can go in,
if they do the right thing, have faith, kiss the stones,
buy holy oil, rub it on the afflicted parts, and pray
for tolerance, as soldiers go by with young voices and big machine guns.

the view from the baby seat

I got here in a thousand cars
humans without cars are sick
the Martian observers said
snails that lost their shells
eighty percent of the world is sick
but they are sick together
when a song makes them amorous or lonely
there is no place they can immediately go

I was once small and scared in my father's
black Packard in the 1950s
everyone was afraid of my father
because my father had a car
I was scared because there was
someone else in the car with us
sometimes there were five or ten
other people in the car with us

I see the invisible passengers
without eyes
without hands
without noses
without bodies
they ride inside our cars
the consummate passengers
the perfect invisible hitchhikers
you don't remember you stopped for
in nineteen-sixty-something

they've been in your car ever since
in all our cars ever since
every one of our cars the nicer
roomier snazzier cars riding up
through the decades like your income
or down it doesn't matter
they don't care
you gave them a ride and they will
be with you forever

what haven't they seen
what haven't they heard
what haven't they felt
what haven't they sniffed
what haven't they licked
everything

the blind guy with exaggeratedly sensitive skin
the deaf guy who sniffs everything
one guy is mostly tongue
one is the Perfect Bad Timing Passenger

some of these specialized pale beings
were picked up by your grandfather
or grandmother and then by your father and mother
in nineteen forty fifty sixty seventy or something
and rode in their cars until your folks died or got too old
to drive anymore and then they moved into your car
and are now in there every time you take the wheel

they are the Perfect Passengers
the Consummate Passengers

they've never spilled anything
they've never said anything

they've never interfered in your domestic squabbles
they said nothing when you were mean to your children
they didn't laugh when you cried
they didn't care when you farted or jerked off
they never questioned where you were going
they just rode along and fed on everything
with the one sense that made the most sense
which is why they live long very long
long enough to outlive you and move
into your children's and your grandchildren's cars
the Consummate Passengers

The blind man who passes his palms
over the velveteen
backseat of the family Impala
where G. poet and friend
drank in the car's exhalation
in his mother's garage
on a dark February day in Detroit, Michigan
where they made the car and broke his father
a dark day in a season of suicides
the sky is a kind of dark mid-70s velveteen
somebody clever said after the funeral
one of those things said inside a car
that only can be said inside a car

The listening guy is not blind
all he does is listen
whatever he hears he hangs on the peg
of these inside-the-car phrases
I told you not to
I told you so
What is that supposed to mean
What's her/his name anyway

If I wasn't going to do this I would
This very minute
I didn't have anything to do with it
They made me do it
That's my business
If they don't shut up right now I'll have to do something
Go ahead and kill me
Do you want to get out right here Go ahead
Can you touch that a little?
Not on your life buster
Can't you see how pretty it is?
It's not real money
What are you looking at you'll get us killed
They are your children too

Years pass everything is recorded

And then there is the Timing Passenger
her job is getting there on time
but her passion is rearranging the incongruous
to produce synchronicity
she's the only one in the car the car likes working with
and loves almost as much as it loves the driver

The Timing Passenger has a nemesis
the Perfect Bad Timing Perfect Passenger
his name is Death and he's thin like cigarette smoke
he survives the folding of the backseat
he lives in-between the squeezed walls of the car
hitting a tree or another car
he's right there his thin shadow between
the bodies slammed like two bronze cymbals
giving up their spirits to the night sky
he's right there in the vw convertible

when the giant redwood looms out of the California night
and kills Jeff and Glenn
and he's in the car when their friends carry their ashes
to the ocean

Oh velour
Oh Chrysler Cordoba Corinthian leather
Oh Japanese limo with swimming pool
Oh Letterman aftermath limo!
This Limo Guy sure knows how to have fun!

I introduce him to distract you from the sadness
of all the Invisible Passengers in your car
for me the best thing is getting out at the light
but I will always ride I will never get out at the light
I can no longer live in pedestrian countries
I am permanently strapped in the baby seat
with all these people around me
Mom and Dad can't see them
maybe they saw them once when they made me in the backseat

The future is a series of better and better furnished wombs
eventually we will not need to leave our cars at all
we will be in paradise and we will be one with glass and chrome and nauga
Look the Martians will say They have cured themselves

JEALOUS WITNESS

INTRODUCTION

• *Jealous Witness*
  Minneapolis: Coffee House Press, 2008 (Editor, Allan Kornblum)

And then it came: 9/11, perpetual war, the militarization of space, the quasi-military state of the New World Order, the destruction of New Orleans by Hurricane Katrina, and the collapse of the world's financial system. Add to that global warming, nuclear catastrophe in Japan, impending environmental energy and water crises, the rise of capitalism without democracy in China. The beginnings of centuries, thinking only of the last two, were not auspicious. The beginning of ours, a milennial century no less, was even more devastating. When my home city of New Orleans was destroyed by bad engineering more than the storm itself, the entire population of one million people was evacuated. One third of its poorest inhabitants never returned. I went back to the city two days after the flood, allowed past the National Guard and army checkposts to report for NPR. Those days, which now stand like a "time outside time," an island of inexpressible memory, were much written about and reported on, but like some of the most powerful experiences of the sixties, they cannot be captured in any media translation. One of the great musical groups of the music city, the New Orleans Klezmer All-Stars, whose members were scattered in cities across America, were determined to return to New Orleans to make the urgent music they felt needed to be made. They asked me to write songs and I did what I do best: I wrote poems for a feverish two days and nights, and the musicians made songs from them. The resulting CD is included in *Jealous Witness*. Any idea that history was at an "end" was abandoned in a hurry: poets have more work than ever.

did something miss new orleans?

what do you call this this catastrophe sonnet
used to be called n'awrleans now it's simply
the greatest engineering disaster in u.s. history
before that it was the greatest human disaster
in pre-civil war history the place to sell slaves
who misbehaved downriver and before that
the greatest rum sugar and human warehouse
in north america the end of the pipe out of which
poured sweet drunkenness and blood and patois
from martinique through the pirate spanish main
before that it was just the greatest swamp a drunk
frenchman ever dedicated to his sun king
so let's rebuild this with new urban principles
that bow to history without throwing up

the mold song

it was one of a kind
the earliest map of the united states
it was hanging right here on the wall
the mold ate it all
in one gulp the mold ate it all
and these books the only copies
of newton franklin galileo
and this shakespeare folio
the mold ate them like they was candy
look at the satisfied grinning mold
stretching from floor to floor
like a fifties horror movie mold
not to speak of that stack of cash
I never shoulda kept around
not a zero left in the whole stack
look at me I'm growing old
I'm giving myself to the mold
it's some kind of lesson
it's some kind of horror story
keep collecting paper things
I knew that one day I'd be sorry
I'm not wearing a mask
I'm not wearing any gloves
I feel stupid I feel cold
I'm giving myself to the mold
halloween and suicide rolled in one

I shoulda sold I shoulda sold
only in new orleans only in new orleans
halloween and suicide all in one
a man of means

in the picture above

for Laura

the graduating class of 1927
portland women's college stands in expectation
of the jazz age above the bed together
with a full deck of your female ancestors
jealous witness of our lovemaking or just
your hello to the past and sorry girls
the thirties are just ahead not that we know
much better what the teens of the 21st hold

topiary

"There are four kinds of people: those who have not been born, those who are living, those who have died, and those who have not been born, are not living and have not died. They are the stars." —mircea cărtărescu

and those who are blossoming in the brain
of a child over and over
born of an understanding
that will not recur after age fifteen but will be forever true
imaginary people with some very good and some very bad traits
many of them with a black eyepatch and a peg leg but always on your side
sometimes these people have to cluster to disguise themselves
in a mercury mushroom holding its form
then they become the fragrant sentries of the floral burst
that is your heart invisible to all but to your loving audience
a heart that will not stop emitting rays of hurt and healing
a mouth murmuring enchantments toward its own self

then at fifteen the prison bars become articulate,
the masked arabesques harden into architectures
oozing soft knowledge, facts, and emphasis.
I've been working on not forgetting
it's no child's play looking all grown up and fooling everybody
gombrowicz was right and so were many other goombas
looks are everything disregard them

the pall descends the pail fills from the deepening well,
time is a racket that swings at the tennis balls of truth,

a wasp nest grows swiftly   a desolate tower
thick with the buzzing of ten million wasps

a deaf bear in a forest cave licks a memory from his paw,
there is a thickness in everything   skin grows muted over skin

they've tacked you like a fabric to the dummy they call reality
unsnapping yourself is no picnic
the logos of unfastening churns unrecorded
a bull-faced cloud peaks just over the horizon

it's death and his gallant five-foot horns capped with steel points
driving the motorized galaxy toward you,
the one slowpoke in the streaming data stream
so gore me with honey and be swift about it

the palliatives of transcendence are the business of the young
who think they know from the screens in their pockets
just who those black-patched peg-legged people are
the screens have recast them in a friendlier style
they seem a whole other kind of people who promise much
whole universes of nothing for little money

when a line of verse escapes the empty wallet
or the heart exulting now and then
heads straight for the sky to bag a passing angel
just doing its job buffing a tired star

the young in the pixel dust are gratified
that the old in their fugitive nobility of ashes
have taken their stories with them
those would have been way too heavy

the unborn people are just around the corner

visitors from the dancing world

the dancers we are about to meet
are fourteen thousand and twenty thousand years old
but look fourteen in their frayed satin slippers no hips round eyes
they have danced a number of universes some of which have exploded
and others have been powered for use by life forms like ours
they visit us because we are one of their earlier creations
they don't use the door they come in the window
or like last time through a crack in the roof
that time they rested their pergament wings
(the same bookbindings are made from)
and danced shut doors trapdoors exits so it would be just them and us
we clunky in felt boots with ice chunks in eyebrows keyboards in hand
histories accounts tacked neatly on walls of empty space we did these things
thousands of years are a long time to wait for dancers
the dancing wu ling masters the sentient motes with skins of brilliant dust
but here they are the darkened air crackles our eyes half-closed taste red
a long time ago their god diaghilev assured them that as long as they
believed in him he would be a window into the lights of the sky and a roof
over their heads a master of luminous dots infusing them with power

as long as they never use the door never never use the door
because he explained eons ago he was a ball of such energy
anyone coming into his house using a door would be incinerated
from his rocker he always faced the door
waiting for trespassers with his umbilical cord plugged in

the sadness of the kind of god I am
he explained cannot be explained

but stick to this simple rule of ingress and egress
and I'll keep you light and fluffy except for those wings
those I have to fashion from pergament
and he wiggled his umbilical and emitted pas de deux and jetées
and now as we flatten in expectation like pages from our favorite books
as his angels fly in, in tight formations of v and Q &
the vanguard are in violet followed by bright carmine and azure
the violet carry two carmines on their backs pulled by one azure
by a thread of gold unraveling behind them
followed by a gaggle of black-clad immigrants from Ellis Island
with steel-weighted suitcases and hearts in canvas sacks
though in fairness some of them have a bubble of happy air
bouncing off a drumskin in their chest so they are already in jerusalem
as unpacked as the dancers no longer heavy with the past
we flatten in expectation of them like pages from our favorite books
they are a crowd with verses trailing them wherever they go
medieval banners unscrolled behind angels in paintings
when we sit down to eat this evening it is for them we fill wineglasses
and we thank them as they land clumsily on the trees and the deck
even when they fail their designated spots they still carry enough otherness
to assure everyone that they and we are not alone that thousands of beings
in flight and in states of luminosity are just a few inches behind and ahead
their heat is generous and communal their bodies slender and available
they are us in our youth and you in yours time hasn't passed
time took some of the others now they are back illuminated
this old age you can have it tonight the landing party lands

walnuts

"I don't like the substances from which poetry is made:
smells too much like ether, like nail polish. You have to
consume your own self too much. . . . The true prose
writer consumes others." —mircea cărtărescu

other than remembering what was designed for forgetting
which is everything even you and other musical works
intended to get your own music going your architecky self
brilliantly described in vast oeuvre of wishful thinking
intended as well as brilliant lagniappe for conquest of others
your nose drinks in the *désuet* perfumes of early works
not so *désuet* as all that in rereading a rather active
angry youth throwing flaming bombs at passing metaphorists
savonarolaishly flinging to hell deniers of other realities
even boring realities identical to ours at moments of actual ennui
the defense of sound distortion through the larynx
of even the least talented a great cause a flag to plant in magma
not a shred of nostalgia anywhere just manly jobs
war demolition damsel-flipping crystal pedagogy aphorism
some of it sloppy broken eggs etc but the sun on the hill city etc
the operations we now see on the big map and admire for strategy
well not really there wasn't any except forward (man) for Poetry
frothed head to foot in spume and steel of youth
then time showed up and the game had a referee a pudgy dude
not that I really cared to find out what I'd done or said
that was all battle and in war all is fair and bloody pink
but I read my contemporaries for clues about the weather
there was clearly more weather than we saw on tv

there were whole countries of weather where a giant cardiogram
was being constructed from the heartbeats of millions hoping for something
there were forests being devoured and air becoming carbon
misshapen channels embodied to broadcast doom that wouldn't leave
even familiar gestures and salutes were clouds of strange
try as you/I/it might you/I or it couldn't make history by ourselves
toys played by the wind are eerie no matter how clever they are
my brilliant contemporaries inscribed mercury drops with scents
that were libraries to dogs who didn't teach them to the hounds of hell
(we did that through metaphor and school)
dogs rolled scents and clues down squiggly country roads
where apotheosis in the shape of a coffee cup rewarded the tired
the sun ahead in the rain-wipers through muted cheers of dying
sometimes cheerleaders in the raindrops caught snacking
audible in the steady rain crunch crunch white teeth
dazzling details of inimitable childhoods looking sadly
similar from inches away that was sad but heck there were colors
gypsy skirts gleeful snotty brats lacquer-shiny bugs in oily rainbows
the terrorists have won by now so kill yourself
the fog is creepy nostalgia the shells thankfully still from lemuria
the world is littered with bodies left behind by you/it/I
who kill selves in more places more times more lines
than I count presently either in your forehead or in the sketch
of the town from above by a fine dutch master each line made of lines
until the field under the cathedral is populated by peasants
and those other shapes are coffins or boats I believe or dragons
with chinese lanterns between their spines like mirabeau bridge
the peasants pop their blossoms or time capsules over their heads
or maybe hats who knew that hats could be such historians
and among all that action the stick figures of museum curators
they aren't yet born but already are very busy collecting
nits and mots from poet stripped thin in walnut covered shore

tristan tzara the man who said no
for kenneth koch

sensibility was not what spelled doom
but rather forelocks and insouciance, palabras y cadavros,
the toasts made ten years before in a cocteau moment.
humiliation and elegance were best of friends for ages.
there were rabbis in the crowds entertaining the slaves.
no one laughed at anything he couldn't kill.
(unless he laughed so hard he couldn't and then he was drunk.)
what we must do now is to conduct the study
of that certain laughter no longer known to us
who laugh without suffering as if laughing was funny.
we'll begin in 1899 when public hangings were thinning out,
long enough to allow for flounces, wit, and mercy.
class, we'll use recordings from the very first chortle
thought worth recording by mr. edison for mr. chaplin.
we'll watch a child before a bicycle in the teens of the 20th century.
upstairs an hysteric laughs before a smoking psychiatrist.
the newspaper with the hole cut in it is full of dire reports.
nobody laughs or even smiles in photographs yet. it won't be
1925 for a long time, and most of the people above are dead.
we have to wait decades before the cost of film allows
co-opting frivolity into the serious business of the world.
furrowed brows, severe bosoms, knotted muscles, epaulets,
modesty, concentration, rigid memorization, eons of duration
hold the well-behaved pause for eternity.
tickled by something in his mind's eye in 1913, a jewish boy
fresh out of the ghetto of moineşti in the kingdom of romania
bursts into a concentrated violence of guffaws before the swiss

releasing centuries of repression and fear combined with a strict
alphabet that until now left no airy gap for youth's springtime
and he does so in public, the war be damned and propriety, too.
he is staring at the nude legs of a mannequin bei in a shop window
and it's cracking him up: her beige ceramic ankles signal
the death of his acquired ancestral gloom.
lenin gives him a look as he ambles toward the library.
death is suddenly upset and sets her minions to work.
we must recover tzara's laugh! we know what happened later.

the incoming sneeze or the old man's nose
self-portrait

cranky old man looking more and more like the devil
in the caricature of a jew by an anti-semite
what are you doing by the pool of anger
with the rotating dresden doll in the black water
and the greek satyr painted on the wine jug
from which you take long sips and then sigh
wiping your mouth with a banana leaf
what up old cat staring into the bottom of your heart
a nose with a flower in it on the verge of a sneeze
you're holding back because you've been told that a revolution
may break out any second and you don't want to annihilate
the combatants with your powerful sneeze and so miss it
even though you know too damn much to romanticize any of that
still nobody can stop you from making trouble
overthrowing the government or any such trick
from your overstuffed bag of poesy snakes gathered on the roads
sucked from the deep seas vacuumed out of dreams
oblique is no more your style than sliced filets of suburban midnight
for you there is always beauty
you can recognize by a whiff like a perfume in a crowd
that's what your crooked nose is for
the effort is great but held in the suspense of your sneeze
worlds pass don't forget to squirt perfume into the air of the malthusian age

desk 07 in the reading room at the british library
june 19, 2003

marx and engels write the communist manifesto at the next desk
08
while at 06
bram stoker is looking over transylvania
in a book
THIEVES OPERATE IN THIS ROOM

above my leather desk 07

lenin at 05
is penning communiqués
his application for a reader's card
under the name jacob richter
has been approved yesterday
and it will end in the permanent exhibit
at the british library
being viewed by andrei and laura codrescu
"richter!" muses laura, "like the scale."
jacob richter who will cause a large-magnitude earthquake
in the world

(in the czech republic a few days hence
the couple is met by a student named geiger
born after the velvet revolution that undid lenin's earthquake
many millions of dead people later)

and a new name is born out of the still-heaving womb of the 20th century:
        geiger richter
a radiation reader who detects seismic activity)

the "memory and mind" exhibition
        at the british museum (until September 23, 2003)

      marx and engels go to the pub
            (they've had a good day on the manifesto)
where they admire the bartender jenny
        karl marx's future wife
           to whom he is already penning
dreadful love poems he is careful to hide from engels
        frau engels expects the men for dinner
           she is fuming the roast is dry
they've been at the pub for six hours
        imagining the future
"the future my ass!" explodes frau engels, "it's that jenny, isn't it!"

      bram stoker goes walking on hampstead heath
         with a boner for lucy
who is already succumbing
             in his mind
to the transylvanian count
        he has just imagined

the future will include jenny and frau engels only for a little while
        and the marxian utopia and the vampire
will go on a long while

the marxian future fails spectacularly after two-thirds of a century
but the Vampire keeps chugging along far from spent into another millenium

THIEVES OPERATE IN THIS ROOM

how true
thieves among whom are future-burglars
         a.k.a. poets
                    imagination workers
poor young in love with waitresses
              and virtuous corruptible lucys
too shy to ever steal anything physically
              not afraid on the other hand
                         to break into the future
                              & clean it out
without as much as an apology to us
              heirs and victims of utopia
                   and vampires

time-thieves and widow-makers
         quietly penning verses

legacy: letters

"j'ai lu tous les livres mais la chair est triste, hèlas"
—mallarmé

"I would like to read, but where are the books?"
—mircea cărtărescu

quoting Mallarmé got you there every time
toltec submarine with dragonfly wings
mating with two or three of your kind on the wet ass
of the beloved floating downstream on a frog floatie
what a beautiful day to be dizzy with happy sun and shimmer
rock of brains built multicolorfully vertical for hawks to cruise
we make days by hand with the aid of god and her trembling fabric
fanfare of buzzing world of slinking lights breaking up in things
to unquote quotes and unmatter matters
surrender at the "hélas" yes we believe that we have
read all the books or that at least we didn't have to
since one who has read them all found in them
nothing better than them & that's as good
as having read them or what else are books for
and I the speaker am not that one but I know her
there is no contest between the them of books
and the them of the flesh we exalt now
a day like this intervenes and all that we knew escapes
and it won't do to ask where it went
it went into things and escaped as small breaths
from the tiny mouths of rodents and frogs and narrow snake ones
or sank into the eyes of an unmoved fly on a leaf

who forgot how she got there
all she knew was that it was time to eat
and that something would soon come close enough
mmm tasty leaf of philosophy
nourishment for many generations
I see no bodies petitioning to embody:
is that a scholar or a fly?
When I was on the leaf books shot out of me
dark moist hélas!
I heard the hawks and wasps and heard songs
her tresses askew
forever mate of a moment in playful sun.
At sunset there was a brief lingering
a yellowing of former self poorly observed
a dimming of exuberance
a marker to put there for the next sunrise
not "a definitive fall" to quote another someone.
The urge to go on dragged out as a soldier is almost as good as sleep.
Believers in iridescent scarab mystery
report news of colors of seasons from old temperate forests
or cities where bricks with bat faces look out on executioners' squares.
A package of their letters smelling like coffee and smoke
is waiting for you at your mail drop in the next town.
Oxygen from mountaintop caves hisses in spirals down to the rooftops
filling with ardor the absentminded students kissing the bark of each other.
The bonbon spheres mix bouquets of evening with wafts of bistro
there is war somewhere but in here no fifth column
the paranoia of knowing oneself having subsided to give way for love,
solid pink, integrity like a cloud in a blue drink,
the shape of the urban future of our city written in lavender ink
on the faces of lovers sparking in starry beds,
tiny demon faces infused with crimson laughter.
See how pretty we dressed the questions up tonight!
I primped the exclamation points and hair-combed the commas

even as children were making rather stark movies about modern times
about themselves and their parents behind the cardboard trees.
I shook the powdered wigs under buggy lanterns
flakes of satire fell
and coleoptera simulating transparency
abrutum tendrae philtrae marstenicum saltunt
(so plant the brutish filter in the arsenic marsh).
Bruitism is a noisy art dead from the city,
an art we invented so that something might speak
when no one will be listening.
My love, I taught you gilded syllables
for the maggoty carnival,
collaboration creaking in its joints begging oil
for its most exquisite corpses,
phosphorus flesh flowing out of bars like piss into gutters.
But that was long ago when I embraced
the metaphorical and the literal under one wobbly streetlight
and cartoon corpses marched under the batons of candor and libido
to a text party like they used to give in the last century.
Now I'm with the fertile and the embodied
And this scattering of text paginating itself for the show
has already marked the moment
now please step out of the way
to make room for people coming in for drinks.
The trapeze has gone off shooting the remaining fools into the sky.
That would be us and the sunrise will be real not tequila.
Hélas so does art trim ranks and teeth
a steady rain on sidewalks and bartops.
That swoosh? The leather wings of generations migrating.
Is it fall already?

the zen post office
for pat nolan

at the zen post office no letters
being sent or received the people
wander in to ask is this the zen
post office and other people there
just to hang out say yes at once
everyone sits down on the windows
where normally clerks stamp
there are no stamps to lick
take a seat by the wanted poster
some of us are writing letters
to people no longer among us
or people we never met or just
invented or are hoping to meet
when they are invented by others
but nothing is being sent plus
the people who look like they are
reading just-received communiqués
are simply looking over at what
is being composed by others
the whole city is like that now
heat and uselessness are drivers
of men and women's wombs

one day I decided to go to work
at the la vie en rose café
the place smelled like sun lotion
and the locals were taking coffee

with cream lots of cream
until noon the café was a sea
of reports and poems being filed
by the waves made by legs being crossed
and recrossed and restless sandaled feet
and newspapers self-importantly creased
items torn noisily out for later
and sudden boys and girls reciting menus
with great concentration and eyes closed
in various accents castilian and welsh among them
the news was dire the menu had not improved
despite the addition of several imported herbs
the sunbathing beauties at the shores of the urban sea
were too far to be seen and too exhausting to imagine
but there was an orchestra across the street
and I was writing it all down with a view to mailing it
from the zen post office above the café
its marine glory as incommunicado as its sister universe

present at the ceremony

art won
there wasn't even a contest
now art is on TV every time you turn it on
you used to say that art is the great enemy
and now it's true
there was a time when that sounded like a joke
made by an artist posed with a cigar between a neon sign for bar
and a monk moon
art is the greatest enemy another drink please
then swaggering home under the monk moon weeping
the technology of the cosmos arrayed itself predictably overhead
as art advanced in the dark on the backs of stealthy products
which entered the mouths of sleepers like serpents
in the morning everyone had strange appetites
they drove fantastic wombs to work and when they got there
work was a game and everybody was ready to play
I have swallowed my reptiles early the police made me do it
everybody else had to wait until the devices became user-friendly
and they put white smoke and sugar on the reptiles

in memory of the 20th century
for robert creeley

not innocence innocents
an unequivocal answer
could only come from an innocent
the guilty hedged their bets
yes those who believe
in the good intentions of others
are the innocents
and when evidence to the contrary
rises from institutes staffed by neighbors
or from their spawn or the newspapers or mail
they are sure that an error was made somewhere
the clerks of heaven are correcting it as we speak
and if they die unconvinced they return as visitors
to take revenge on their own naiveté and innocence
these are the saddest visitors of all

the tourist towns are strung like pearls
along the coasts and on the peaks
they thrum they glow in the minds of tourists
lugging an ocean of myth in brochures
heavy as mountains of longing
palm pilots full of internet sadness
churches cafés sex clubs on cliffs or caves
blood quickens in an agglomeration
of postcards of ancestors smothered
by desire to return ectoplasmatical and refashioned
from their old countries with advice and smoked sausages

full of idealized landscapes
they've cried enough enough in their saucy graves
they are back on a tidal wave of yearning
ready to sell the little kitschy things they made while dead
they are themselves tourists visiting their living descendants
who now take them home and hang them like flags from rafters
warning figures of continuity to bums without origin or any vagabond
who might mistake tourism for comedy or something local
or offer an insult in the form of money or some other rude crude
eventually the clan shreds and tatters fly (it is windy

funder acknowledgment

Coffee House Press is an independent, nonprofit literary publisher. Our books are made possible through the generous support of grants and gifts from many foundations, corporate giving programs, state and federal support, and through donations from individuals who believe in the transformational power of literature. Coffee House Press receives major operating support from the Bush Foundation, the Jerome Foundation, the McKnight Foundation, the National Endowment for the Arts—a federal agency, from Target, and in part, from the Minnesota State Arts Board through the arts and cultural heritage fund as appropriated by the Minnesota State Legislature with money from the Legacy Amendment vote of the people of Minnesota on November 4, 2008. Coffee House also receives support from: several anonymous donors; Suzanne Allen; Elmer L. and Eleanor J. Andersen Foundation; Around Town Agency; Patricia Beithon; Bill Berkson; the E. Thomas Binger and Rebecca Rand Fund of the Minneapolis Foundation; the Patrick and Aimee Butler Family Foundation; Ruth Dayton; Dorsey & Whitney, LLP; Mary Ebert and Paul Stembler; Chris Fischbach and Katie Dublinski; Fredrikson & Byron, P.A.; Sally French; Anselm Hollo and Jane Dalrymple-Hollo; Jeffrey Hom; Carl and Heidi Horsch; Alex and Ada Katz; Stephen and Isabel Keating; the Kenneth Koch Literary Estate; Kathy and Dean Koutsky; the Lenfestey Family Foundation; Carol and Aaron Mack; Mary McDermid; Sjur Midness and Briar Andresen; the Rehael Fund of the Minneapolis Foundation; Schwegman, Lundberg & Woessner, P.A.; Kiki Smith; Jeffrey Sugerman; Patricia Tilton; the Archie D. & Bertha H. Walker Foundation; Stu Wilson and Mel Barker; the Woessner Freeman Family Foundation; Margaret and Angus Wurtele; and many other generous individual donors.

NATIONAL ENDOWMENT FOR THE ARTS

This activity is made possible in part by a grant from the Minnesota State Arts Board, through an appropriation by the Minnesota State Legislature and a grant from the National Endowment for the Arts.

MINNESOTA STATE ARTS BOARD

TARGET.

To you and our many readers across the country, we send our thanks for your continuing support.

Good books are brewing at coffeehousepress.org